I0754848

You're In Good Company

THE ART OF FRIENDSHIP,
MOTHERHOOD, AND SHOWING UP

ASHLEE GADD

COFFEE + CRUMBS

ZONDERVAN

You're In Good Company

Published by Zondervan, 3950 Sparks Drive SE, Suite 101, Grand Rapids, MI 49546, USA. Zondervan is a registered trademark of The Zondervan Corporation, L.L.C., a wholly owned subsidiary of HarperCollins Christian Publishing, Inc.

Requests for information should be addressed to customercare@harpercollins.com.

ISBN 978-0-3104-6711-3
ISBN 978-0-3104-6707-6 (audiobook)
ISBN 978-0-3104-6713-7 (eBook)

Author is represented by Jenni Burke of Illuminate Literary Agency, www.illuminateliterary.com.

HarperCollins Publishers, Macken House, 39/40 Mayor Street Upper,
Dublin 1, D01 C9W8, Ireland (https://www.harpercollins.com)
Cover design by Gabriella Wikidal
Interior design by Kristen Sasamoto
Photography by Jennifer Floyd

Printed in Malaysia

25 26 27 28 29 30 VPM 10 9 8 7 6 5 4 3 2 1

Do not forget to show hospitality to strangers,
for by so doing some people have shown
hospitality to angels without knowing it.
HEBREWS 13:2

I wanna cook for people and make them happy
and give them the best bacon on earth.
CHEF SYDNEY ADAMU, *THE BEAR*

Contents

Introduction

ASHLEE GADD

One of the best gifts I ever received was a box of Cheez-Its left on my porch.

Still in the fog of grief after my miscarriage, trapped in a world of black sweatpants and Netflix numbing, I was curled up in bed, sandwiched between a stack of pillows and a heating pad, when my friend Anna texted.

Checking on you. Please choose from the following options.

A multiple-choice list followed: (1) Anna could pick up my two older kids and watch them for the afternoon, (2) she could send dinner via DoorDash, (3) she could grab anything I needed from Target and leave it on the porch, or (4) she could offer up prayers and good vibes, with no tangible services rendered.

I couldn't help but smile. Anna has always excelled at friendship, showing up in swift, practical, and specific ways. Without hesitation, I accepted her third offer—the Target concierge—and asked her to bring me a box of Cheez-Its. Apparently, my pregnancy craving hadn't caught up with the fact that I was no longer carrying a baby. Then I sent her a picture of an empty toilet paper roll and asked if she could grab more of that, too.

An hour later, a box of Cheez-Its and a package of toilet paper appeared on my porch like magic. Like Anna. The second I opened the door, tears welled up in my eyes. *This is friendship*, I thought. *This is what it looks like to put skin on your love.*

How often do we overcomplicate these things?

Friendship—female friendship, in particular—can sometimes feel elusive and mysterious. We open Instagram and see girls' trips and birthday dinners and images that conjure up Mindy Kaling's famous question (and the title of her book): *Is Everyone Hanging Out Without Me?* We are desperate for deep, meaningful friendships, the kind that get better with time, but our expectations don't always match reality. We want to attract good friends and keep good friends and *be* good friends, but . . . how? What's the secret sauce?

On paper, what I received from Anna that day might not seem like much—a box of Cheez-Its and a dozen rolls of toilet paper—but to me, it was everything. I felt seen and cared for. I felt so, so loved.

When was the last time you felt that way?

When was the last time you made someone else feel that way?

Maybe it's been a while, on both accounts. Maybe you've felt more invisible than seen lately, more unknown than known. Maybe you recently started a new job, moved to a new area, or welcomed a new baby into the fold. Maybe you're rebuilding your life and figuring out who your people are, *again*. Or maybe you're simply in a rut, longing for deeper friendships but not sure where to start. Maybe you're somewhere in between, in a liminal space of sorts.

At Coffee + Crumbs, our online storytelling community for moms, we've been writing about motherhood for over a decade. If we've learned anything during that time, it's that mothers are hungry for connection. They are also—always and forever—hungry for stories that make them feel safe, known, encouraged, and loved.

We come to you in these pages with arms outstretched, humbly offering a full plate of our trials and triumphs, all the ways we've gotten friendship wrong and all the ways we're trying to get it right. This is a book about gathering and making space, not just for bodies and plates and conversations, but also for vulnerability, belonging, empathy, communion, and love.

This is a book about flinging open our doors as well as our hearts.

This is a book about flinging open our doors as well as our hearts.

This is also a book about . . . *food.*

Before we go any further, I need to disclose something about my personal culinary skills. Every time a meme circulates on Instagram about eating cereal for dinner, at least fourteen people send it to me. That is not hyperbole.

My family can confirm: I am not—nor have I ever been—a whiz in the kitchen. While I can certainly whip up tacos and spaghetti and the occasional box of Kraft Mac & Cheese, I'm also the one perpetually assigned "dinner rolls" at Thanksgiving. I feel the need to confess all of this at the very beginning because putting together a collaborative book with recipes (!) is both laughable and extremely off-brand for me.

Having said that, *a girl's gotta eat.*

Even someone like me can admit the undeniable, ever-present, significant role that food plays in both friendship and hospitality. When I think of every celebration, every loss, every beautiful and broken moment in my life—not to mention the millions of ordinary ones sprinkled in between—food was there.

Funfetti cupcakes for my son's first birthday.

Salty truffle fries dipped in ketchup at a much-needed girls' night out.

Piping hot minestrone soup served with warm focaccia bread during a period of grief.

When we're happy, we eat. When we're sad, we eat. When we feel none of those things, we still have to eat. Food is an entry point, a common ground, a simple yet profound language of love. This shared reliance on food and drink is part of what makes us human and connects us to one another. We break bread because we need to, because our physical bodies require nourishment to get out of bed, and also because we want to, thanks to a creative God who generously gifted us with taste buds that crave and respond to dishes both savory and sweet.

"When in doubt, bring food" is a mantra that works for just about anything. We use food to comfort, to celebrate, to console, to offer something tangible when we don't know what to say. When we feed people, a hidden part of us is also fed—that tiny part of our heart that longs to nourish others.

Jesus Himself used food in miracles, in parables, and in the holy sacrament of Communion. It is impossible to read about water being turned into wine and empty nets suddenly bursting with fish—not to mention thousands of people being fed with mere scraps—without concluding that *food matters*. In the same way Jesus met spiritual needs by way of addressing physical needs, we, too, can use food as a gateway to something greater.

Sometimes food looks like making things with our hands: slicing an onion, grating a block of Parmesan cheese, cracking eggs, and kneading dough. Other times, food looks like sharing tacos on a patio, grabbing a box of donuts en route to the park, or delivering containers of chili on

Christmas Eve. From home-cooked meals we prepare ahead of time to store-bought snacks we grab in a pinch, these are stories about feeding people and being fed, not for the sake of performance but for the sake of presence.

This is a book about food, but it's also about the stuff *underneath* the food. We're writing about roast beef sandwiches and sugar cookies and arugula salad, yes; but underneath the recipes and ingredients, you'll find a plethora of other things: compassion and care, generosity and grace, tenderness and love.

This is a book about friendship, but not the kind that hangs out in the shallow end. We're talking about the real, honest, raw, nitty-gritty parts of making and keeping friends. Patience. Forgiveness. Consistency. The art of showing up and going first, imperfectly, again and again and again.

Finally, this is a book about hospitality, but not the Pinterest-perfect version. While we can certainly appreciate a beautiful aesthetic, our end goal here is not a long wooden table covered in burlap, featuring an elegant mix of taper candles and fresh eucalyptus in Mason jars. Our end goal is, simply put, to create a culture of welcome. After all, hospitality can happen anywhere and everywhere, from driveway fire pits to living room floors covered in Magna-Tiles.

There is no secret sauce here.

If anything, *you* are the secret sauce.

We hope this book nudges you to pick up your phone and call or text a friend. We hope these pages beckon you into the kitchen, to chop bell peppers or stir risotto or make lemon cake from a box mix. We hope this book makes you feel encouraged and expectant for what opening your home can look like, for how friendship can flourish with just the tiniest of seeds.

Between physical gatherings being swapped for the convenience of Zoom, ultra-filtered Instagram reels, and AI being incorporated into everything we do, it's no wonder that so many of us are grappling with a distorted sense of community against the backdrop of a distorted sense of reality.

We wrote this book to help us remember what it's like to embody friendship.

We wrote this book to help us put skin on our love.

While we put forth every effort to make this book beautiful, please know that we don't wish for it to stay that way. We want this book to shuffle back and forth between your nightstand and your kitchen counter. We want you to actually make these recipes and share them with someone you love. We hope these pages end up dog-eared and highlighted and splattered with tomato sauce. We hope you feel inspired and equipped to start a book club, supper club, Bible study, or playgroup. We hope these stories fill you with hope, faith, and the confidence that you are perfectly capable of creating the community you desperately want to have.

We wrote this book to help us remember what it's like to embody friendship.

This is not a book you read. This is a book you *live.*

As always, we'll go first.

A Blessing Before You Read

KIMBERLY KNOWLE-ZELLER

You're in good company here—
with friends and mothers,
daughters and sisters,
aunties and grandmothers,
dreamers and creatives,
helpers and believers.
Come in and take a seat.
We've been waiting for you.

We see you—
the ones peering through the
    door afraid to knock,
the ones watching other
    mothers talk and laugh,
the ones stumbling through
    the recipes,
the ones up late googling your
    child's latest symptoms,
the ones ordering pizza (again),
the ones rocking babies and
    shuttling children to practice,
the ones in need of a friend,
the ones in need of a hand.
We've been waiting for you.

You're in good company here—
as you are fed
and as you feed others.
Pull up a chair;
there's always room for more.

You're in good company here—
with your baby purees,
first bites of avocado and eggs,
grilled cheese and quesadillas
    (again),
homemade food and takeout,
frozen corn dogs and
    chicken nuggets,
produce from the garden,
and freshly baked bread
    delivered from a neighbor.

You're in good company here—
whether you're using fine china
  or paper plates
or have unfolded laundry
  scattered across the
  living room.
It doesn't matter how you dress
  or how much mail is piled in
  a corner;
what matters is that you're here
  and welcome,
as holiness and grace seeps
  into the nooks and crannies
  of the table
and cradles you in the soft
  couch cushions.

You're in good company here—
when the days are rushed
and nights are filled with long
  conversations.
Come and join us at the table,
where highs and lows are shared,
school days are recounted,
family vacations planned,
prayers are spoken,
forgiveness is offered and
  received.

You're in good company here—
with your unmade beds and toy-
  strewn living rooms,
the dirty dishes lining the sink,
with friends who know they don't
  have to knock
but walk in and say,
Let me hold the baby,
I can wash that for you,
the ones who text,
Thinking of you,
Here's to a new day,
I'm here for you,
the ones who send
the memes that make you laugh
  out loud
and the jokes that only you
  understand.

Here's to the friends who
  wrangle toddlers
and change diapers and
  exchange meal plans,
the ones who show up with
  Goldfish and coffee,
the ones who push your stroller
  for you,
the ones on the sidelines
  cheering with you and
  worrying through the night
  until teenagers come home,
the ones who know your coffee
  order without asking
and follow up that you made
  that call.

You're in good company here—
come in and take a seat.
The water is cold, and the coffee
is hot;
this seat right here is just for you,
to feel the comfort of a blanket on
your lap,
to watch your child be rocked
by another mother,
to sit and be and take a breath.

Come in, we've been waiting
for you.

Wherever you are,
whatever you have,
however you feel,
come and see,
take and eat,
there is a place for you.
You're in good company.

1

A Few Simple Ingredients

KATIE BLACKBURN

The first time I try the salad is at one of our yearly college reunion get-togethers at the river. Every summer since graduation, we fill a big house with anywhere from ten to twenty-five friends, and all our kids get sunburned out on the boat. We eat a huge dinner and stay up way too late telling stories around the fire, reliving the memories we've all retold a dozen times because they still make us laugh until we cry twenty years later.

As the kitchen fills up that special evening, with hands ready to help and small bellies demanding to be fed, I see Emily pull out the biggest bowl she can find in the kitchen and dump a Costco-sized carton of arugula in it. Then she swirls good olive oil all over the greens and squeezes lemon juice, turns the salt and pepper shakers more than one might think is sufficient, dumps a few generous fistfuls of Parmesan on top, and sticks two salad tongs in the mix. In three minutes, a beautiful bowl of salad is on the counter and being heaped onto paper plates next to salmon and hamburgers and corn on the cob.

"Emilyyyyy!" I say through a mouthful of peppery and tangy bliss. "This is to die for!"

"Isn't it so good?" She smiles back. "It's my favorite salad in the world. And it is the easiest thing you'll ever make, Katie. You cannot mess it up; it's always just right."

I go back a few minutes later for a second helping, but the entire Costco-sized package of arugula Emily made into a salad is gone, leaving only a dusting of Parmesan and olive oil at the bottom of the bowl. Perhaps we are an exceptionally hungry group of friends, but really, I think Emily's salad is just that good.

Thankfully, Emily brings her arugula salad to every dinner we share together for the next three years.

I met Emily when we were freshmen in college, at a campus ministry for student athletes. She was a superstar basketball player who looked like a real-life version of Disney's Princess Jasmine: tall and athletic and strikingly beautiful, with a laugh and personality that warmed the temperature of the room from the moment she walked in. I was the opposite in almost every way: short and average, shy and unremarkable. But as soon as I met Emily, I felt drawn to her like a magnet. I wanted the warmth, the encouragement, the magic her personality brought wherever she went.

It started simple, as most friendships do: We met for lunch at Dilly's Deli on Arizona State's campus. I was recovering from knee surgery and getting around on crutches, so Emily carried my turkey sandwich from the counter to the table for me; then she cleared all the leftovers when we'd finished. I've never forgotten what it felt like to have someone I was just getting to know carry everything I couldn't—and do it with joy. But Emily has always seemed to know how to carry things for people.

We grew as friends, catching up in the computer lab during our required study hall time, meeting up for frozen yogurt, and attending each other's games when our schedules allowed (basketball for her, soccer for me). We talked about being followers of Jesus on a secular college campus, and we shared the physical and mental load of being student athletes and carrying the pressure of performance in all areas of our lives. We also loved working together with our campus ministry and formed the group of friends that would gather at the river twenty years later.

Emily and I lay by the pool for hours in the Arizona sun and ate our way around Tempe's best cheap college spots. Emily and her fiancé once set me up on a truly hilarious and terrible double date, one that involved sushi and bowling and perhaps too much to drink (the date, not me). I have never let them forget that night and the comical catastrophe it was.

We built memories like little bricks in the home of our friendship, one at a time. Those four years of our lives—so fun, so full, so remarkable at forcing us to learn what we were capable of—were a season we often long for, wishing we had another chance to savor it.

My ex-husband's struggle with addiction came to a breaking point a few months after our tenth wedding anniversary. For me, discovering his addiction was not only shocking, but the shock amplified the pain. The same day the secrets came to light, he went to an inpatient recovery program for the first time, a Monday in December. The hurt, the wild incongruity of life from one day to the next—it felt impossible to make it through the day.

Emily came over to my house the afternoon I found out, with chicken pot pie for me and pizza for the kids, and, of course, the ingredients for her arugula salad. And four days later, on a Friday afternoon, she texted me: *I'm coming over for a sleepover. You can't say no. I have brownies and popcorn.*

She walked in the house the same way I remember her walking into the room the night I met her in college—joyful, energetic, full of life—and the temperature changed. She helped me put my six kids to bed, and then we sat on the couch with our warm brownies. And because I was empty and spent and out of words, we let our silence and tears fill the space. She slept on my daughter's bed so I wouldn't be alone in my house that night. And she knew me well enough to tell me I couldn't say no to her presence or her snacks. It was as if Emily knew intrinsically, as author Ann Hood once wrote, "That even in grief, we must take tentative steps back into the world. That even in grief, we must eat."[1]

Here's the thing about my friendship with Emily: It's sturdy and solid, with all those bricks of laughs and disagreements and apologies and *Can you believe that happened?* memories in the foundation, but it's never been perfect. We've been insensitive and had arguments and have misunderstood each other more than once. But the difficult moments make a friendship just as strong as the good ones. And when you're standing on something you trust is built well, it tends to need less maintenance in the long run.

The difficult moments make a friendship just as strong as the good ones.

That's why when Emily moved across the country, from Spokane to Atlanta, I wasn't worried about us. Over two decades of friendship in our busy lives, we had become experts at making five-minute phone calls, leaving quick voice memos after school drop-off, sending slightly inappropriate and always hilarious GIFs, and not worrying about the stretches of silence in between—because, bless it, sometimes Emily takes a week to respond to a text. One time she apologized for not responding for a few days, and I told her, "It's okay, Em, I know you are giving your whole self to whatever is right in front of you."

And she is. She's done it for me a thousand times.

Some friendships in my life need more than five minutes here and there; with other people I think *I* need more than that, perhaps because we share less history, fewer memories to rely on, a shorter catalog of hurting one another's feelings and needing to ask for forgiveness without knowing how that rocky patch will end. People don't often tell you that a good friendship needs a record of wrongs made right to be strong, but it does. And I don't think those conflicts are always bad, because when two people want to restore something, it is usually stronger than before.

Friendships built during different seasons will have different foundations, and the foundation determines everything. But just like Emily's arugula salad, our friendship has a few simple ingredients: memories, loyalty, understanding, and trust. It's quick, easy, and reliable.

And after all these years, it's really hard to mess it up.

My husband spent four months in a recovery program, and for the next two years, I thought we were both working as hard as we could to restore what had been fractured. But nothing about addiction is simple or predictable.

My marriage ended for good on a Wednesday. And Emily wasn't just a few miles away anymore. She couldn't come over with dinner and salad and dessert and her determination to make things better. And of course, processing the fresh grief of such a huge loss in my life needed more than our five-minute phone calls in those first few days; one morning, we talked while I cried in the Target parking lot for thirty minutes .

But as the weeks went on, as my appetite came back and I found my footing, I started making Emily's salad for lunch a few days a week. It was like I was taking tentative steps back into the world. A few handfuls of arugula, a splash of olive oil and lemon juice, some salt and pepper, everything topped with Parmesan. After a quick toss, I'd sit on the couch with my feet curled under my body and eat. The routine was a comfort and a good choice for my healing body. Mostly, in this season of loss, it was an embodied reminder that something in my life remained constant.

On a particularly quiet afternoon at my house, with five kids in school and one taking his nap, I texted Emily as I sat down to eat her salad. It always makes me think of her and reminds me of the strong, solid bricks of love and care I have around me. She responded to my text in her quintessential Emily way, with a deep question that gets to the heart of how I'm really doing: *Tell me something you're proud of yourself for, Katie.*

I wrote back lightheartedly: *Eating this salad instead of a milkshake right now!*

A few more silly exchanges, and then we were back to our lives, to the dishes and the children and, for me, the healing.

But in those few moments, my friend carried me, helping me with the heaviness of a season that hurt, just as she's been doing since the first time we had lunch together. And I couldn't help but feel the weight come off me just a bit. I smiled and thought about what a grace it is to have long friendships, quick phone calls, trust in the distance, and arugula salad.

Emily's Arugula Salad

I already know what some of you are going to say: "I don't like arugula." Fair enough. I'm glad you know yourself. And I wish I could tell you that a spring mix or a bowl of spinach or kale would produce the same result with this salad, but alas, I cannot. The peppery bite of arugula is the magic to the simplicity here. You're welcome to try another green, but please, don't say I didn't warn you.

MAKES ABOUT 2 ENTRÉE SERVINGS OR 4 SIDE SERVINGS

- 1 (5-ounce) package fresh arugula
- Extra-virgin olive oil to coat the greens
- Juice of 1/2 to 1 lemon
- Salt and black pepper to taste
- 1/4 to 1/2 cup freshly grated Parmesan cheese
- Toasted slivered almonds, optional (if you're feeling fancy and craving a crunch)

1. In a large bowl, add arugula.
2. Drizzle the greens with olive oil, just enough to coat them. Squeeze in fresh lemon juice.
3. Add salt and black pepper to the mixture.
4. Sprinkle Parmesan over the greens, then toss the salad together. Taste the greens, adjusting the olive oil, lemon juice, Parmesan, and seasonings to your liking.
5. Sprinkle with toasted almonds, if using.
6. Enjoy during naptime when the house is quiet, if possible. While you eat, text a friend and ask her to name something she is proud of herself for doing.

2

How Can I Get Them to Stay?

MOLLY FLINKMAN

When my eleven-year-old daughter, Lily, asks if she can make sugar cookies on a Saturday afternoon, the answer is an easy yes. I grab our stepladder and pull my well-worn handwritten recipe card out of a high cabinet. We preheat the oven together, and then I take a seat on a stool at the counter, content to watch her complete all the steps herself.

She unwraps the margarine, and I remind her that this specific kind of margarine is one of the reasons why these cookies are so good.

"Why does it matter?" she asks.

"Actually, I'm not sure," I say.

I came about this cookie recipe the first year my husband, Jake, and I were married. One of my childhood friends had tucked the recipe card in a wedding gift bag alongside all the required nonperishable ingredients. I mostly followed the recipe the first time I made the cookies, except I used margarine instead of butter, and I skipped the step instructing me to chill the dough for two hours. I didn't want to wait that long, so I rolled the warm dough into small balls and figured I'd see what would happen. The cookies were so soft and delicious—made even better with a thin layer of vanilla icing—that I never got around to following the recipe as it was originally intended.

Since that day, I have made countless batches of sugar cookies for people in my life. I've brought them to professional development meetings, church potlucks, and baby showers. I've sent them to work with Jake and made them for parties—whether or not we were hosting. They're a bit of my legacy is what I am trying to say. When people see them plated on a counter, they know who made them. They almost always eat more than one.

But today, while I'm watching Lily cream the sugar and margarine with our hand mixer, I find myself thinking about the future teenagers I will make these cookies for someday—the future friends who will be looking for a place to hang out together on the weekends. Someday after a basketball game or before a school dance, they'll need a place to go, and I want them here. What's more, I want them to *want* to be here.

I'll bribe them with these cookies, I think. *This is how I'll get them here.*

But then I consider what I have to offer them besides warm baked goods. I start with our couch, because what teenage hang is good without a couch? Ours was given to us almost a decade ago, though it certainly wasn't new then. Brown and threadbare, it sits in the center of our family room, which suddenly seems small and unexciting when I imagine it full of lanky kids. Here on my stool in the kitchen, I think about all the things our home *doesn't* have to offer: There's no backyard pool here. We don't have a fancy movie room. We don't have a finished basement. In fact, our 1939 farmhouse basement doesn't even have the potential to be fully finished. When I take it all in, our home tends to feel crowded and a bit bedraggled.

But some things are new here. Jake recently replaced most of the flooring on our first floor, and I have been slowly chipping away at updating the light fixtures. These are nice touches, but when it comes to our house, my eye always seems to be drawn to the shabby and unfinished—the three colors of trim in most rooms, the holes in the wall by the back door, the piles of papers I can't seem to figure out how to stay on top of.

Our menagerie of old and worn things doesn't feel like much to offer our kids' friends someday. I worry they'll want flashy technology and nicer spots to gather. I want them in our home, but what do we really have to give them? I can bake them these delicious cookies, sure, but is that really enough to make them stay?

I watch Lily measure and mix, measure and mix—adding the wet ingredients and then the dry—and I think about when I was a teenager, back in the early aughts. My friends and I traveled in a large coed group in those days. We hung out together most weekends, and we'd decide whose house to go to through a combination of landlines and early Nokia cell phones.

My friends' basements and family rooms varied in size and style, but many of them were dark and arguably too small for a crowd our size, which could sometimes reach a dozen. A few of our chosen spots had room for only a loveseat and a corner recliner. We were often splayed across the floor and got pretty good at squeezing together on sectionals. But never once did we care about amenities. We were not concerned about the size of the television or the make and model of the refrigerator. All we cared about was being together.

Usually, before we would pile into someone's basement, we would hang out in the kitchen first, where moms and dads would feed us and pepper us with questions. Our school was small, so our parents had all become friends, too. While we were on courts and fields, they were on bleachers and sidelines, rooting us on together. I couldn't tell you the color of the walls in those homes or whether any of the carpet had recently been replaced, but I do know that our collective group of parents loved us. We crammed around their tables and filled their driveways, and every set of those parents was completely delighted to host and serve us. We were everybody's kids, and we knew it.

I have long since wanted to re-create this for my own kids—this sort of pack mentality and communal friendship experience—but now the state of our home gives me pause. I wish I had more to offer these hypothetical future teenagers.

Once Lily is finished mixing, she rolls the dough into balls just like I've shown her time and again. I help her slide the cookie sheet into the oven, and then she sets the timer and escapes into the other room while I start to clean up.

I wonder when I started to care about all the tiny imperfections of our home so much—when I started to wish for more and new and bigger and better.

I wasn't always this way. When Jake and I were first married, I loved our apartment décor, a hodgepodge of hand-me-down items from our childhood homes and college dorm rooms. There were a few new pieces sprinkled in from our wedding registry, but those things didn't reflect a cohesive sense of style. Nothing really matched. One of our couches was made of a faded blue-and-gray plaid fabric, and the other was deep pink with a kick pleat skirt around the base. The couches sat in front of our television stand, which was actually a desk Jake had sawed in half and turned backward in the corner. And yet none of it fazed me. None of it bothered me the way it all seems to bother me now.

I grab a dishrag and start to clean the counters.

I think it all shifted when I started to notice how other people in my life have homes that could be magazine features. These homes have well-designed entryways; they have places to file the mail and the one million papers the kids bring home from school. There are no handprints all over the walls. There aren't random single socks scattered around the rooms. The trim is painted the same color. There is a cohesion in these homes that has slowly made me feel self-conscious about the seeming mismatch of mine.

The timer goes off, and Lily bounds back into the kitchen. I watch her carefully move each cookie to the piece of parchment paper I've set out on the clean counter. We mix the frosting while the cookies cool and then dip each one into the shiny glaze.

I hope they'll keep coming back because they know how much we love them.

And it's this small moment that resets something for me. This simple act of togetherness—of connection between the two of us—reminds me that I'm paying attention to the wrong things. Maybe some kids care about fancy things, but I think most just want to feel known and cared for. At least, that was true of my pack of friends. It's true of Lily right now. I like to believe it will be true of the future teenagers who will walk through our door someday. And when I think about it that way—about how I can best love our kids' friends when they're here with us—the state of our couch suddenly feels less important. I'll never have a keen eye for design, but I do know a thing or two about how to make people feel welcome.

That's enough, I tell myself. It's a simple shift in focus, but it makes all the difference. It re-centers me on what actually matters.

"I'll make these cookies for you and your friends someday," I tell Lily while we stand there in our imperfect kitchen—holes and handprints and all.

I'll make this recipe for our kids' friends any time they want, and maybe they'll come for the cookies. Maybe this is how I'll get them here, but I hope they'll keep coming back because they know how much we love them.

Lily and I each take a cookie. They're slightly underbaked to perfection.

"It's just right," I tell her, and it is.

Best Sugar Cookies Ever

Set aside everything you thought you knew about sugar cookies. This recipe doesn't require chilled dough or a rolling pin, and it isn't going to give you flat cookies. Instead, you're going to bite into a soft ball of sugary goodness and never look back to the old way of things. These cookies pair perfectly with any occasion: parties, potlucks, holidays, and regular weekday afternoons. Just heed my one warning: Do not overbake them.

MAKES ABOUT 24 COOKIES

For the sugar cookies

1 cup vegetable oil spread, softened to room temperature
1 cup granulated sugar
1 egg
1 teaspoon vanilla extract
2 teaspoons baking powder
3 cups all-purpose flour

For the icing

2 cups powdered sugar
1 teaspoon vanilla extract
1/4 cup milk

For the sugar cookies

1. Preheat the oven to 400 degrees.
2. In a large mixing bowl, cream the vegetable oil spread and granulated sugar with an electric mixer until light and fluffy, about 2 minutes. With the mixer on low, add in the egg and vanilla, and mix until incorporated. Add in the baking powder, and then mix in the flour, 1 cup at a time, until fully combined.
3. Roll the dough into 2-inch balls and place 2 inches apart on an ungreased cookie sheet. Bake for 8 to 10 minutes, then check the bottom of the cookies. If they are golden brown, take them out of the oven. Do not overbake. Transfer the cookies to a wire rack or parchment on a counter, and let them cool completely.

For the icing

1. While the cookies are cooling, in a medium bowl whisk the powdered sugar, vanilla, and milk until thoroughly combined. If you want a thicker icing, add more powdered sugar.
2. Once the cookies have cooled, dip the top of each cookie in the icing so that one entire side is covered. Place each cookie on parchment paper so the icing can set.

Note: In place of vegetable oil spread, you can also use butter or margarine. But for the best flavor, I recommend vegetable oil spread—particularly Imperial Vegetable Oil Spread.

3

Once Upon a Time

CALLIE FEYEN

Once upon a time, I was in the best book club that ever was. It consisted of three members: my friends Rae and Emily, and me, Callie. When we met once a month, we called our meetings "REC days" because of our initials and also because a lot of times our meetings took all day, like a good recreation day ought to. We began at Colorado Kitchen, a place in Washington, DC, that served the best coffee and donuts the city had to offer. After a hearty book discussion and breakfast, we moved on to whatever adventures we had planned. We rode our bikes along Rock Creek and through the National Zoo. We ate lunch at Politics and Prose. We ran around the terrace of The Kennedy Center. We drank beers on the banks of the Potomac.

We read *A Tree Grows in Brooklyn* and decided we had to stand in a New York City tenement where the protagonist, Francie, grew up. So we did. We drove to New York City and walked up a narrow, creaky, dark wooden stairwell and thought about Johnny, Francie's father, coming home after a day's work, singing his favorite song, "Molly Malone." We stood on old floorboards and looked around at the dark, tiny space and wondered about seeds that are planted in a great big city.

Once, during a trip to the annual Maryland Sheep and Wool Festival in West Friendship, Maryland, the three of us were watching sheep get sheared up to their chinny-chin-chins, and we all decided we needed to learn how to knit. Rae told us about a lady named Helga who, word on the street of the nation's capital, was the best knitter in all the land.

"I know she'll teach us," Rae said as the three of us watched a farmer lead a sheep to be sheared. A bluegrass band played in a barn nearby, a tune about heartache and pain set to banjos and a fiddle. The sheep's hair fell in puffs to the floor, as if it were a part of the tight-knit harmony.

"Helga's blunt," Rae said as we stared at the sheep, now bare. She didn't say it like she was warning us. Rae spoke like we were getting free French fries with our meal. "She tells the best stories," Rae said, and the farmer led the sheep away, and the band played on.

Helga agreed to teach us, and Monday evenings became knitting nights. That first night, she led us to a nook built into her yellow kitchen, where three woven baskets holding skeins of yarn were waiting for us on the table. "That's my yarn, and those are my baskets," she told us. "And you can keep them."

We each took a seat at the table, and she showed us how to cast on, making the first loops of yarn on the needle. Rae and Emily got it right away, but all I did was tie knots; my fingers were so tangled in the mass of yarn and needles, it looked like I was giving the finger to knitting.

"I'm left-handed," I muttered, looking at the floor.

Helga shook her head. "Nuh-uh, honey. Left-handed ain't got nothin' to do with it." She slapped a hand on my shoulder and leaned in. "You got to bloom where you're planted." She looked at my fingers, the tips turning purple from the yarn that was wrapped around them. "Honey, I think this is the wrong soil."

She started to laugh. I looked at Rae, who was struggling to keep a straight face.

Emily looked at me with her lips set and her eyes slightly sympathetic but more matter of fact, as if to say, "Helga's right."

I laughed so hard that I was afraid I would have an accident if I didn't get my hands untangled and get myself to Helga's bathroom.

I think Helga questioned my intelligence because I kept coming back for knitting nights. I brought my basket and my knotted-up yarn and I pretended to try while I listened to Helga tell her stories. She had a story and a comeback for everything. She could talk about politics, faith, marriage—nothing was off-limits, including the story she told us about the time she knitted a bikini. Whatever happened in that bikini was scandalous and precisely what Helga had intended to have happen, but Rae, Emily, and I were laughing so hard at the concept of a knitted bikini that I barely remember the rest of the story.

What I loved about Helga's stories—about Helga—is that she wasn't there to teach us a lesson or impart wisdom about what it means to be a wife, a woman, a good Christian girl. Her stories were gifts, pink packages with silk bows she handed to us. We were all too eager to pop off the top, look inside, and ask, "What will we do with this?"

"Whatever the heck you want," Helga would say.

The last time I saw Helga was the spring of 2008, when I went to her house for a bridal shower for Rae. I was about six weeks pregnant, but I was bleeding, and it wasn't stopping. My ob-gyn knew what was going on and told me to come in that Monday "to make sure." She didn't say anything else, and I didn't need her to. I knew what would happen next.

Somewhere women are always telling stories to each other. The stories are often told in the dark—maybe in a cave or, more likely, while waiting for the Metro. The darkness and the waiting, they're important. Because usually that's where the stories come from. "This reminds me of . . ." one of the women might say. Or, "Here's how it happened . . ." It's in the darkness that "once upon a time" is born, a rope that tethers women together if we are brave enough to hold on. Somewhere, right now, women are telling stories—on the soccer field sidelines, in coffee shops, in the carpool line, around a firepit or an old dining table draped with a wine-stained linen cloth hiding marks of life imprinted on the wood: pencil indentations from homework, rings from hot tea mugs, scratches from plates heavy with something homemade, something shared.

That spring day, when buds from the cherry blossoms were just beginning to burst, I went to where the stories were. Not because I wanted to forget my own, but because I needed help carrying it.

I put on a black dress with silver skulls for buttons and a high slit. I had bought the dress in New York City with Rae and Emily. I'd bought it because it was edgy and nothing I'd ever pick out to wear, but I loved the way I looked in it, and I loved the way I felt—strong and confident. I slid on black heels. The dress had a belt, and I tied it around my waist loosely because I wanted to be gentle with whatever small seed might be trying to grow in the dark.

At Helga's, I sat around the table with Rae and Emily and a slew of other women and listened to stories, mostly told by Helga. She told us about growing up in Germany, living through World War II, and marrying an African American soldier, then moving to the United States during a time when interracial marriage was banned.

That spring day, when buds from the cherry blossoms were just beginning to burst, I went to where the stories were.

She used to sell Avon, and most everyone thought it was a little side job—something to do in between chores and childcare. Helga's husband got sick, and among the sadnesses they were dealing with, they could no longer go to the beach and swim as they used to every year. "We should build a pool in our backyard," Helga told him. He said they had no money for a pool. "Maybe you don't, but I do," Helga said. Over the years, she'd squirreled away a dollar here and there and had saved over ten thousand dollars—enough to build a pool in the backyard.

"First thing I'm gonna do when I get to heaven is find that man," she began. "Second thing I'm gonna do is smoke a cigarette."

"Anything else?" Emily asked.

"I'm gonna find God. I have some questions."

Day turned to early evening, and wind blew through Helga's open windows. Her white curtains lifted and rustled, making a few of her porcelain trinkets shake. Helga, who was well into her seventies, made a move to begin clearing the table, but Rae, Emily, and I beat her to it. She followed us into the kitchen, though, and as we rinsed off dishes and loaded them into the dishwasher, we chatted on like four besties.

Helga asked Rae what she would do next, after she got married, and Rae said she would continue to teach, at least for a while.

"Mm-hmm," Helga said and looked at me knowingly. "You can't do it all," she said and winked at me. I'd left teaching two years earlier because I was pregnant with Hadley. Sometimes I wish I had the courage to tell Helga that I wanted to know how to do it all, that I spend most of my days resisting the idea that I must give something up in order to be good enough for something else. *When will I learn time management, Helga? When will I learn to say no? What is a healthy boundary?*

Rae scooped dish detergent from a green box under the sink into the dishwasher and started the machine. She told Helga about the giant school building the principal was planning on constructing.

"He's comparing it to the promised land," Rae said.

"The promised land?" Helga said, squeezing out water from a knitted dishrag. She turned to face us and leaned against the counter.

"So he thinks he's Moses?" she asked. Emily, Rae, and I laughed.

"I guess," Rae said.

"Someone ought to tell him Moses never made it to the promised land," Helga said and slapped the rag on the sink, nice and neat.

Helga might not have been able to teach me how to knit a scarf, but she taught me how to knit a story by following whatever yarn catches my eye, no matter what anyone else might say about its worth. Casting on might've proven detrimental to my fingers, but I learned how to fling myself into the world, offering up what I have, like the sheep who stood silently while the bluegrass band played their high lonesome songs and we all clung to what we knew of sorrow and pain and what had fallen, in the hope it could be picked up and something new could be made. Helga showed me how to make something bloom.

And she taught me how to listen for whatever story was on its way next. Two days after I stood in Helga's kitchen, I walked into the sonogram room, resolved for whatever "once upon a time" was to happen next.

I heard a heartbeat—its pulse so loud it filled the room like the Tenebrae drum on Good Friday, its thump fierce and beautiful and terrifying and making room for a brand-new story.

No-Burden Bread

I have a knack for making everything complicated. No matter what it is, I find a way to sprinkle confusion, extra steps, even mayhem wherever I go. This is probably one of the reasons Helga knew I shouldn't knit. So when I found a recipe for what I can only call a "sourdough hack," I assumed it was too good to be true. This bread is so easy to make, I daresay you'll throw out that Mason jar of sourdough starter that's been in your fridge since—be honest—the pandemic.

MAKES 1 LOAF

3 cups plus 2 tablespoons all-purpose flour, plus more for dusting
1 3/4 teaspoons kosher salt
1/2 teaspoon quick-rising yeast
1 1/2 cups water

1. In a large bowl, mix the flour, salt, and yeast.
2. Add the water and, using a dough whisk or a wooden spoon, stir until a shaggy mixture forms and pulls away from the mixing bowl.
3. Cover the bowl with plastic wrap and *walk away*. Seriously! Let this bad boy do its thing on the counter for about 12 hours. I usually make the dough the night before and bake it in the morning.
4. When you're ready to bake, preheat the oven to 450 degrees. When the oven has reached 450, place a lidded cast-iron skillet (or Dutch oven) in the oven. Heat the cooking vessel for 30 minutes.
5. While the cooking vessel heats up, pour the dough onto a heavily floured surface and shape it into a ball. Cover the ball with plastic wrap and set aside.

6. After heating for 30 minutes, remove the cooking vessel from the oven and drop the dough inside, without the parchment. Place the lid on top, move the cooking vessel back to the oven, and bake for 30 minutes. After 30 minutes, remove the lid and bake an additional 15 minutes, until the bread is golden and baked through. One way to determine it's fully baked is to flick the loaf to make sure it has a nice hollow thud. Remove the loaf from the oven and place it on a cooling rack. Slice when you're ready to eat.

Note: This recipe is adapted from the *Simply So Good* blog by Janet Barton.[1]

4

Keep Showing Up

SARAH J. HAUSER

I knock softly a few times with my left hand, balancing a tray of food on my right. My friend's husband opens the door and welcomes me into their home. The screen door slams shut behind me.

"Come on in," he says with a smile, gesturing toward the kitchen. "Thanks so much for the meal."

The aluminum pan I'm holding tips a little too far forward. *Oh no!* I think, but thankfully I regain control before the entire meal splatters on my friends' kitchen floor. He takes the warm tray of grilled chicken from my arms and puts it on the counter, and I set a paper bag holding plastic containers of green beans and brownies next to it.

"You're welcome!" I say, then quickly add, "So, how's it going?" That last phrase leaps from my mouth—a bubbly, high-pitched, nervous reflex spoken before I can snatch it back. I hang my head. "Sorry, dumb question," I say, trying to recover.

My friends have just suffered a miscarriage. What did I expect him to say?

"We're okay, I guess." He shrugs.

We enter the living room where his wife sits, a blanket wrapped around her legs and a tissue box on the side table next to her. She looks tired, deeply weary. My eyes focus on a spot on the floor. I know that if I look at her, I'll cry and probably make things worse, or I'll offer a cliché comfort that surely won't help. I want to step into their pain, to feel their ache, to help hold the weight of their grief. In order to do that, though, I have to fight the instinct to ease my own discomfort by filling the silence with empty words.

My friends are generous and kind, and they brush off my awkwardness. I sit on the couch and listen to them share how they are *really* doing. No fake smiles or platitudes. We cry together and pray together, pressing gently on the most tender parts of their grief. As hard as it is, I know how much moments like these matter—moments where we let grief spill over onto others so they carry the heartache alongside us.

As hard as it is, I know how much moments like these matter—moments where we let grief spill over onto others so they carry the heartache alongside us.

But when I get in my car to drive home, the second-guessing begins. *I can't believe I was so annoyingly perky when I showed up! Were the questions I asked too personal? Did the chicken taste too dry? Was I more of a nuisance than a help?*

Minutes ago, my heart had been breaking for them, but somehow, in the fifteen-minute drive back home, I had turned my visit from being about supporting *them* to focusing on *me*.

Over a decade ago, during my mom's battle with cancer, I started regularly flying from Chicago, where I lived, to New Jersey to help my parents however I could. Mom had declined to the point where she was receiving in-home hospice care and was almost entirely bedridden. Thanks to a flexible job, I was able to sit in the wingback chair in their bedroom, right across from the hospital-style bed my mom now inhabited, with laptop in hand and coffee next to me. I was "working from home" eight hundred miles away from my apartment.

In between sending emails and writing reports, I answered my parents' phone and played gatekeeper—the family receptionist. These were the days of landlines and answering machines, so there was no option to set the phone to vibrate or Do Not Disturb while Mom slept. I told friends and family whether she was up for a visit, what she could eat at that point for those who wanted to bring food, and if my dad needed anything. I let people know when either of my parents felt too exhausted to talk, though I always promised I'd pass along their messages.

As my mom's health continued to decline, her ability to talk and visit declined as well. She slept most of the time, her eyelids often involuntarily closing mid-sentence. She couldn't get out of bed at all anymore, and her only movement came when we lifted her up to shift her body to keep bedsores to a minimum.

The moments when Mom was awake felt like a gift, and I was determined to take advantage of every lucid second. We'd talk about her pain level, how Dad was faring, who had called while she was sleeping. One afternoon, after I hung up from yet another phone call, I walked across the hall, back into her bedroom. Her hospital bed was tilted slightly upward, and her eyes were open. This was one of her "good" moments, so I asked how she wanted me to handle the growing number of calls and requests to visit. "Is the phone waking you up too often? Do you want me to tell people to stop calling?" I asked.

I straightened the blankets on her bed and lifted her water cup to her lips so she could take a sip before responding. I felt unsure of what to do. I couldn't heal her cancer. I couldn't take away her pain, and I couldn't even make her a meal since she was barely eating. I felt antsy and sad and uncomfortable sitting in the quiet without the ability to "fix" the problem.

Others who loved her felt the same way. Friends from church offered to bring dinner. Aunts and uncles wanted to know the latest doctor's report and how they could help from afar. Women from her Bible study asked if it was okay to visit. We all wanted to *do* something. But at that stage, there wasn't anything, really, that we could do. And so, I wondered if the phone ringing and the knocks on the door and the requests for updates were all too much for her.

"People keep asking me if they should call or not, because they don't want to burden you," I added. "What do you want me to tell them?"

I knew she'd give me an honest answer. By this point, almost two years since her diagnosis, I'd gone with her to chemotherapy and oncology appointments. I'd helped bathe, dress, and feed her. My siblings and I had asked my parents hard questions and talked openly about their finances, their will, and what the final moments before Mom's death would be like. After our lives had been rubbed raw by cancer, there was no need to hide behind a pretense of politeness. If she needed me to tell people to stop calling, that's exactly what I'd do.

Her hands were folded over her stomach, and her eyes closed softly as she responded in a near whisper. "I'd rather people call and not be able to talk," she said, "than lie in bed wondering why the phone never rings at all."

I once dropped off one of my favorite meals to another friend going through a hard time, and the minute I set the Tupperware containers on her kitchen table, I started apologizing. I'd made that meal a hundred times before, but when I taste-tested it, it just wasn't as good as usual. I had been running late so I didn't have time to remake it. I handed her the food, and the words started to tumble out of my mouth: "I hope it's okay! I'm sorry I'm late! And I'm so sorry if the meat is too dry!"

Other times when visiting friends in crisis, I've said the wrong thing, filling silences with unhelpful words. I've overcooked chicken and woken up babies with the sound of the doorbell. My words have rushed past their suffering and tried to tie up their story in a bow instead of pausing long enough to see and sit with them in their pain. Or I've sat in my house doing nothing, because their grief felt so big and my capacity so small that I've wondered whether sending a measly text message to say I was praying for them or a note of encouragement even mattered.

With every question, every doubt, every bit of second-guessing pinging around in my brain, my offerings so often have become about *my* performance and how *I'm* perceived, rather than about seeing and serving others. And too often, I so fear doing it wrong that I never show up at all.

But loving someone well requires letting go of the fear of our own failures. If we're going to be there for people in hard times, at some point we're going to get it wrong. Yes, we should make an effort to provide the best, most helpful support we can. But despite our best intentions, we will often miss the mark. We're left, then, with two choices: (1) sit quietly in the fortresses of our own homes, thinking it's the only surefire way to avoid mistakes, or (2) choose to keep showing up, however we can.

There's a lot I don't remember from those years my mom was sick. I don't remember what people said when they called, if they sounded annoyingly cheerful or asked intrusive questions. But I remember sitting in a desk chair next to Mom's bed, holding my laptop toward her as I read every single Facebook comment from people who knew and loved her. I remember the sweet, smooth vanilla custard Mrs. Smith brought over—the only food my mom could eat toward the end. I remember people we hadn't talked to in years—including, I came to find out, an old flame from before she married my dad—writing the kindest words on her CaringBridge page. I remember my dad having a stocked freezer and family friends who provided a catered dinner for over fifty people the night before her memorial service. I remember a woman from Mom's Bible study picking me up from the airport, another couple bringing us sandwiches at the hospital, others who prayed faithfully. I remember my dad setting stacks of cards on the kitchen island and, with tears in his eyes, saying, "Can you believe this? Can you believe all the cards we got?"

And I remember that the phone never stopped ringing.

Sometimes the act of showing up for others is a whole lot simpler than we make it out to be.

Sometimes the act of showing up for others is a whole lot simpler than we make it out to be. It's not about bringing the perfect dinner or having the right words to say. It's not about the questions and doubts that fill our minds after dropping off a meal. It's not about us at all.

Showing up is about making sure no one feels forgotten. It's about truly seeing people—in their pain and their celebrations, in their mourning and rejoicing. And it's about loving others, in both grand ways and small gestures, using whatever our hands and feet and minds and hearts have to offer.

Grilled Chicken and Peach Skewers with Lemon-Basil Dressing

After I had twins, we were the grateful recipients of all kinds of delicious meals. But the one I remember most was a simple dish with grilled meat and produce. This recipe is one of my favorites to make for others. It's gluten-free and dairy-free and can be easily doubled. I serve it with whatever starch I have on hand—like a quinoa salad, roasted potatoes, grilled corn, or sweet potato fries.

MAKES 4 SERVINGS

For the skewers

- 1/2 cup olive oil
- 1/4 cup freshly squeezed lemon juice (about 1 lemon)
- 1/4 cup chopped fresh basil, plus more for serving
- 3 tablespoons honey
- 1 tablespoon lemon zest
- 3 cloves garlic, minced
- 1 1/2 teaspoons kosher salt, divided
- 1/2 teaspoon freshly ground black pepper, plus more if desired
- 2 1/2 pounds chicken breasts, cut into 1-inch cubes
- 4 to 5 ripe peaches, cut into thick wedges
- Wood or metal skewers

For the skewers

1. Add the olive oil, lemon juice, 1/4 cup basil, honey, lemon zest, garlic, 1 teaspoon salt, and black pepper to a large zip-top bag. Zip the bag securely, then shake well to mix.
2. Open the bag and add the cubed chicken to the marinade. Zip the bag securely and shake the mixture again so the marinade evenly covers the chicken. Marinate in the refrigerator for 2 to 8 hours.
3. When you're ready to cook, if you're using wooden skewers, soak them in water for at least 30 minutes before using so they don't burn.
4. Preheat a grill or cast-iron grill pan to medium-high heat. Remove the chicken from the marinade, letting the excess drip off. Discard the marinade.
5. Thread the chicken and peach wedges onto the skewers, alternating one after the other,

For the dressing

$^{1}/_{4}$ cup mayonnaise

2 tablespoons freshly squeezed lemon juice

2 tablespoons chopped fresh basil

1 tablespoon honey

Salt and pepper to taste

until all the ingredients are used up. Sprinkle the chicken and peaches with the remaining $^{1}/_{2}$ teaspoon of salt and a bit of black pepper if desired.

6. Cook the skewers for 5 to 7 minutes per side or until the chicken is cooked through (to at least 165 degrees). Transfer the skewers to a serving platter and drizzle on the Lemon-Basil Dressing (recipe follows). Garnish with additional fresh basil.

For the dressing

1. In a small bowl, whisk together the mayonnaise, lemon juice, basil, and honey until the mixture comes together. Season with salt and pepper to taste. Drizzle over the skewers. Feel free to make the dressing a day or two in advance, storing in the refrigerator until you're ready to use.

Note: Peach slices that are especially ripe have a hard time staying on the skewers. If that's the case, then I skip putting the peach slices on the skewer. Instead, I slice the whole peaches in half (removing the pit) and grill the peach halves separately from the chicken.

5

Church of the Firepit

MELANIE DALE

We had no idea what we were building all those years ago.

We walked around the outside of the house, through the yard to the back, down the stone steps, avoiding the one that wobbled, and took up positions around the fire pit. Eight chairs, grouped into four couples. I held my breath from the driveway until we all sat down, unsure of the rules, nervous about air and breathing and particles of mystery virus. All of us looked haggard, thrust into working from home while homeschooling, with the constant threat of literally coughing to death, rationing toilet paper, and a new two-can bean limit at the grocery store. I probably—no, *definitely*—made a joke about beans and toilet paper.

We came with travel mugs of tea and "tea" and water bottles and coolers like roller suitcases. BYO–whatever got you through. We listened to music and stayed late into the night, tears of laughter streaming. We loosened up and poured out the stress and fear. We felt normal again.

By the time we each made our way back home, we noticed something had lifted and we'd forged something important. So our gatherings became weekly. Every Saturday, after the young babes laid down their sweaty heads and the old babes settled in to watch movies, we grown-ups met around the fire for laughter and whiskey and jokes about *Tiger King* and the latest headlines. Someone insisted that the pandemic would be over by May. It wasn't, so we kept showing up.

I dubbed us "Church of the Firepit."

Life slowly ground forward and our pack ventured out of our neighborhood. Eventually, soccer games and swim meets and work trips pulled us in different directions. But we kept meeting together as often as we could, rotating who hosted. We became "Firepit," whether we were around one or not.

My phone somehow decided fire pit is one word and capitalized, though it still autocorrects *jammies* to *Jammie's* 100 percent of the time. "Firepit" isn't a place. It's a body of people, an *ekklesia*, a community.

I learned about the importance of building a community from my parents. Every Sunday night, my brother and I would lie on their bed and watch *In Living Color* on a portable black-and-white TV with an antenna sticking out of the top while my parents had their people over for Bible study. Mom would bake brownies or cookies and brew a pot of Folgers and make spiced tea on the stove. Their friends would show up and every now and then laughter would trickle up the stairs, or we'd hear my dad's voice sharing something while the Fly Girls danced on our tiny TV.

The other day, I called my mom to ask where she got the recipe for spiced tea and caught my parents driving home from apple picking. I heard the smiles in their voices as they reminisced about getting invited over to a couple's home after church when they were newlyweds, back when Dad was in vet school and before they had me. They spent the afternoon playing cards with friends and drinking spiced tea.

To me, community still smells like coffee and spiced tea. As soon as the chill of fall creeps into the air, I pull out my mom's spiced tea recipe, mulling cinnamon and clove on the stove, making the house smell so good. The tea simmers as friends arrive and tastes great out of a thermos around the fire pit or ladled from a simmering pot on the stove.

About a year and a half after the inception of Firepit, after countless mugs and memories and the recognition that we'd become so much more than friends, I found out I had breast cancer. I told our Firepit family first, and before my first surgery, they surprised me with a breast cancer party, with fancy craft cocktails and homemade cake and gifts exclaiming "[*Bleep*] cancer!" They created the perfect playlist of all my favorite nineties tunes, and we sang around the fire pit into the night air, with the crickets as backup. They nailed the perfect ratio between praying for me and leaning into boob-themed gifts.

> **To me, community still smells like coffee and spiced tea.**

Toward the end of chemo, when my immune system came back, I drew on my eyebrows for the first time and returned to Firepit, feeling like a boiled chicken and nervous to have other people view my Baldilocks. They were so kind. They were so safe. They exclaimed how good my eyebrows looked, and I decided to believe them.

We've continued to show up for each other, through highs and lows, in sickness and in health, dropping off porch meals and driving one another's kids. What a gift to experience community at your lowest and discover nothing but love and support.

Our conversation usually weaves between sketches on *Saturday Night Live* and hilarious things our kids said, to our anger with the Church and the sometimes-devastating realities of our marriages or families. These days, even though we're less worried about catching mystery germs, we still BYO-whatever, but we usually bring enough to share, sipping scotch or bourbon or spiced tea.

At times, we've shared Communion around the fire pit, passing a plate of crackers and a bottle of red wine and taking turns reading Bible verses off our phones. To some it might be weird or sacrilegious, but to us it's connection. The bread, the wine, the "doing this in remembrance." Maybe over time Church of the Firepit really has become a church. We certainly seem to pray a lot.

Recently, one of us texted in our group chat first thing in the morning: *Guys, I just called 911.* Her husband had passed out or had a seizure. She thought she'd lost him. Just a regular day that suddenly threatened to destroy her whole life before she'd even had breakfast.

With barely an eye open, I read the text three times before typing back: *Praying. Oh my gosh. We're here. We love you.*

The chat exploded to life, everyone adding their prayers and offers of help. The nearest couple helped get their kids to school while they went to the hospital. While our friend underwent all the tests the hospital had to offer, the rest of Firepit used the group chat to put together a dinner menu. Throughout the day, we dropped off snacks, appetizers, sides, a main dish, and dessert.

This is what community looks like.

Our friends went home from the hospital that evening. As they sat around the dinner table, exhausted but grateful that everyone was alive, stable, and well-probed, their middle child looked at the meal before them and observed, "This is what community looks like." Our kids see it, just as my brother and I saw it all those Sunday nights when we were kids.

At Firepit, we love one another and we fiercely love one another's kids. Our kids are *ours.* Yes, they're ours, as in each individual family's, but they're also *ours*, as in the collective Firepit's. Firepit's fourteen kids have a wide age spread with lots of overlaps. When our first kid reached his senior year, we did the math and realized that, for the next many years, Firepit has a kid or two or three graduating each year. We show up and send off and party and pray for the graduate. We probably could've bought one set of graduation cards with gift cards inside and just passed them around.

We agonize together and we celebrate together as our kids make big decisions, make bad decisions, break records, and break our hearts. We love and defend our Firepit babes, whether they're home learning to ride a bike or traveling around the world, drinking milk or drinking beer.

Tonight is Firepit. And as my husband arranges the logs in the fire pit and sets out the eight chairs in a circle, I fill a pot with water, set it on the stove, and pull out the ingredients for spiced tea. They're easy, regular ingredients that I pretty much always have on hand. Like spiced tea, the ingredients for community are simple, everyday things. Just show up and build it, one log on the fire and cup of tea at a time.

Spiced Tea

Nothing says welcome like a warm mug in your hands. I start making this as soon as we hit the "-ber" months every fall. People swear there's apple in this tea, but it's citrus and spice! You can make this with regular tea bags or decaf. My mom uses bottled lemon juice, but I like squeezing real lemons. Use whatever you have on hand. It's delicious either way.

MAKES 12 TO 16 SERVINGS

- 1 gallon water
- 2 cups granulated sugar
- 1 teaspoon ground cinnamon
- 1 teaspoon ground cloves
- Cloth bag for steeping spices
- 4 black tea bags
- 1 cup frozen orange juice concentrate
- 1/2 cup lemon juice

1. In a large 6-quart stockpot, pour in the water, add the sugar, and bring to a boil.
2. Place the cinnamon and cloves in the cloth bag and add to the boiling water. After 5 minutes turn off the heat.
3. Add the tea bags. Let the mixture steep for 5 minutes.
4. Remove the spice bag and tea bags. Add orange juice concentrate and lemon juice.
5. Stir the tea and ladle into mugs.

6

Good Mothers Bake from Scratch and Other Lies I've Believed

ASHLEE GADD

I am standing at the kitchen counter, spooning banana mix into a muffin tin, when my daughter makes a proposal.

"How about dis . . . ?" Presley begins, pausing for dramatic effect. "How about I put *four* chocolate chips on each muffin because dat's how old I am?"

I smile at her logic. Once every pink polka-dotted liner is filled with batter and topped with exactly four chocolate chips, I place both tins on the middle rack and set a timer. Presley runs out of the room and returns with her plastic step stool, placing it directly in front of the oven. I watch in amusement as she takes a seat and stares at the dirty tempered glass like a television.

"I'm gonna watch da muffins bake," she tells me.

The boys are at basketball practice tonight, which means we've got the whole house to ourselves. Per Presley's request, our girls' night agenda includes baking, watching *Beauty and the Beast*, and painting our nails. Before we move on to the movie and manicure portion of our evening, I return the vegetable oil to the cabinet, put the carton of eggs back in the fridge, load the mixing bowl and spatula into the dishwasher, and finally, toss the cardboard box that once held the muffin mix into the recycling bin.

It's the last step that haunts me for a second. The box mix. The shortcut. The scam. A trace of guilt flickers in my chest as a tiny voice in the back of my head reminds me: *Good mothers bake from scratch.*

I swat the lie away, but it comes right back like a boomerang, ready for a debate.

Obviously real bananas are superior to a packet of powder, nutritionally speaking, but the aesthetics win, too. Baking from scratch involves a multitude of steps, kitchen gadgets and tools, visible remnants of flour and sugar smeared across the counter. When you're done baking from scratch, you're left with a noticeable mess to clean up: evidence of your time, your energy, and of course, your love.

A box mix, on the other hand, is a quick fix. The drive-thru of culinary offerings. One bowl, one plastic pouch of beige powder, usually water or oil, and perhaps a single egg. In the end, there is no mess left behind. No evidence of time or energy or love. No evidence of anything at all.

The batter practically makes itself. Like magic. Like . . . cheating.

"Eating is serious business," my grandmother would remind us every time we sat down to eat at her dining room table. At Grandma's house, we did not play with our food or lean back in our chairs or complain about whatever mystery meat appeared on our plates.

Ironically, for all the proclaimed seriousness around mealtimes, my grandma also had quite a sweet tooth. She never served dinner without the promise of homemade dessert, and for the entirety of my childhood, I anticipated my grandma's Christmas fudge just as much as the presents she'd bring. Every year, she'd fill two metal tins with individually wrapped chocolate fudge: one with nuts and one without. (The nut-free batch is how I knew she loved me—because I was a kid, and nuts were gross.)

Freshly baked treats and fudge aside, when I think of Grandma Georgia, or "Georgie" as my grandpa calls her, I mostly think of the signature breakfast she prepared every time I slept over: chocolate waffles.

Before you picture Grandma Georgia donning a floral apron, blending flour and cocoa powder into her porcelain white KitchenAid mixer, I should clarify that chocolate waffles contain only two ingredients: (1) a toaster waffle and (2) Hershey's chocolate syrup. And before you picture those bougie "healthy" protein waffles we have today, I should clarify that I'm talking about straight-up Eggos, as in "L'eggo my Eggo," as in those delicious frozen yellow discs you can throw like a Frisbee. As for the Hershey's chocolate syrup, yes, I am referring to the kind you put on ice cream sundaes.

The recipe couldn't be easier: Toast the waffle and drizzle generously with chocolate syrup. By "generously," I mean every single divot on the waffle should be filled to the point of overflow. If the waffle isn't completely soggy by the end—breaking under the weight of sheer decadence—you're doing it wrong.

To this day, I do not recall ever seeing a trace of guilt on my grandmother's face when she served me a nutritionist's what-not-to-eat breakfast. I only remember delight in her eyes and a sly smile as she reminded me, "Ashlee, eating is serious business."

When my grandparents begin the process of what I can only call end-of-life decluttering, I ask for exactly two mementos: the cherrywood upright piano and my grandma's vintage KitchenAid mixer.

In the same way I occasionally purchase a new notebook assuming it will unlock some kind of undiscovered writing genius within me, I take my grandmother's mixer believing—or perhaps hoping—that owning such a quintessential kitchen appliance will magically transform me into the ideal mother I have always wanted to be: the mother who bakes from scratch.

(This same mother also possesses the selflessness of Mother Teresa, the stylish eye of Joanna Gaines, the fashion sense of Gigi Hadid, and the organizational chops of Marie Kondo. It's possible I struggle with unrealistic expectations.)

In my defense, occasionally I *do* bake from scratch. I've been known to whip up scones to fight off the winter blahs, and sometimes I bake chocolate chip cookies when I get writer's block. Sometimes I bake when I simply feel like it, when a genuine desire bubbles up inside my chest to create something with my hands.

Other times, though, I bake from scratch out of sheer guilt, driven by a sense of obligation, insecurity, or some toxic inner pressure I feel to keep up with the Instagram trad wives and perfect sitcom moms.

No matter what lures me to the kitchen, though, the after-feelings remain the same: Baking from scratch leads to a flicker of pride while baking from a box leads to a flicker of shame.

Am I the only one who feels this way?

As it turns out, this particular form of baking guilt can be traced back a few generations. In 1933, John Duff's gingerbread cake mix was the first of its kind, offering women convenience in a box. Big flour mills and other companies quickly jumped on the bandwagon, and by 1947, shoppers had spent $79 million on cake mixes.[1]

After flying off the shelves for two decades, box mix sales began to slow in the mid-1950s. Desperate to understand the shift, General Mills hired Ernest Dichter—a psychology and marketing expert—to investigate why. After interviewing women and exploring how their emotions connected to the art of baking, Dichter reported that using a box mix felt self-indulgent. In order to be proud of a cake, women needed to feel as if they had really baked it.

This research spurred new ads framing the cake mix as merely one step of many. *Add frosting and sprinkles! Cut a hole in the cake and fill it with canned peaches!* Magazine articles encouraged readers to see the true art of baking as something that happened after the cake came out of the oven. The possibilities were endless; women just needed to add their own creative fairy dust. Sales took off again.

Today, the cake mix industry is valued at over $1 billion,[2] but it's not without stigma. In her book *Something from the Oven*, food journalist and historian Laura Shapiro writes, "To this day, guilt follows many of those boxes home from the supermarket the way Jiminy Cricket followed Pinocchio—his conscience always with him."[3]

In other words, while cake mixes are still a modern convenience, they never lost their reputation for being second-best or their association with cheating.

Ten years ago, maternity clothes and baby gear shuffled in and out of my house like library books. Back then, just as one friend would deliver a baby, someone else became pregnant. My inbox held a constant slew of baby shower invitations, registry links, and of course, Meal Train calendars.

As a grateful recipient of two postpartum Meal Trains myself, I dutifully committed to bring dinner to every new mom in my orbit. And even though I had two little kids at home and could hardly put a nourishing dinner on my own table, I fulfilled every Meal Train sign-up by cooking from scratch: chopping, slicing, blending, pounding, frying, and occasionally almost burning whatever Pinterest recipe du jour I had printed that day. Sweaty and stressed, I'd drop off the meal, then head back home to clean my disaster of a kitchen at peak witching hour, often before pouring bowls of cereal because I forgot—or was too exhausted—to double the ingredients.

For so long, I viewed shortcuts as a form of cheating, but what if shortcuts are actually a form of grace?

After the birth of my third baby, a friend signed up to bring us a meal and offered to grab our favorite takeout. *Name the restaurant*, she texted. *Tell me your favorite thing on the menu, and I'll drop it off at 5 p.m.*

I will never forget staring at my phone, dumbfounded, processing this new-to-me permission. *Wait a second. It's okay to sign up for a Meal Train and drop off food you didn't make from scratch?*

I had no idea this was an option.

That would be amazing, I texted back, along with a sandwich order from my favorite deli.

It had never occurred to me that the old adage "fed is best" could apply to mothers, too. But food is food. Dinner is dinner. With that perspective in mind, homemade casseroles and pizza deliveries are equivalent gestures of love.

For so long, I viewed shortcuts as a form of cheating, but what if shortcuts are actually a form of grace? What if shortcuts free us up to serve more often and—even better—with a more cheerful heart?

The phrase "from scratch" originally referred to the starting line of a race scratched into the ground, a visible mark where all runners could begin from the same spot. For so long, I viewed baking from scratch as an even and fair starting place, whereas baking from a box represented a head start. One method is good and true; the other is straight-up cheating. One is evidence of your love, and one is evidence of your laziness.

Yet my own grandmother—who made chocolate fudge and plenty of other things from scratch—is the same woman who unabashedly served me Eggo waffles with chocolate syrup. Did one offering matter more than the other? Did one make me feel more loved than the other?

The chocolate fudge takes ten minutes of prep, twenty minutes to make, three hours to cool. Chocolate waffles take forty-five seconds. And yet, I undeniably felt loved and nourished by both. More than thirty years later, homemade fudge and chocolate waffles reside equally in my brain as warm memories connected to my grandma.

Tonight, pulling banana muffins made from a box mix out of the oven with my daughter, I am learning to see a similar story. Sure, we took the easy way tonight, although I guess you could say we added our own creative fairy dust in the form of chocolate chips. My daughter is happy. The muffins are delicious. This shortcut blessed our evening and freed up more time for manicures and a movie.

The phrase "from scratch" also has another meaning: "from the beginning." When I feel a sense of guilt creeping up, as I still do sometimes, I am trying to remember that nourishing people through food is a form of love, no matter how it's made or how much effort is involved. As in, sometimes I bake from a box and sometimes I bake from scratch.

Either way—from the very beginning, I was thinking of you.

Georgia's Famous Fudge

Look. I don't even like fudge. I only like this *fudge. If your kids, like mine, don't love nuts, you can use that pickiness to your advantage here. Make a batch* without *nuts if you want to share with your kids; make a batch* with *nuts if you want to keep more for yourself. Be warned though: Once you start eating this, it's hard to stop!*

MAKES 64 PIECES

- 4 cups mini marshmallows
- 1 cup granulated sugar
- 1 tablespoon instant decaf coffee crystals
- 1/4 teaspoon salt
- 1/4 cup margarine
- 2/3 cup evaporated milk
- 1 (12-ounce) package semisweet chocolate chips
- 1 teaspoon vanilla extract
- 1 cup nuts, chopped, optional
- Petit four or mini muffin cups, for serving

1. Prepare an 8 x 8-inch baking pan by lining it with foil, adding a little extra foil on two sides so you can easily lift out the fudge later. Spray the foil lightly with cooking spray.
2. In a medium saucepan, combine the marshmallows, sugar, decaf coffee crystals, salt, margarine, and milk.
3. Set the pan over medium heat and stir constantly until the mixture comes to a boil. Let the mixture boil for 5 minutes, stirring constantly to prevent burning. (Do not skip this step—*it really needs to boil for 5 whole minutes*! Something to do with science. Don't ask me to explain it; just trust me.) Remove from heat.
4. Add the chocolate chips. Stir until the chips have melted and the mixture is completely smooth. Stir in the vanilla and chopped nuts, if using nuts. Pour into the prepared pan.

5. Leave the pan on the counter for 15 minutes to cool, then move to the refrigerator for 2 to 3 hours, or until fudge is hardened. Once the fudge is cool and firm, lift the foil from the pan and place the fudge on a cutting board. Using a very sharp knife, slice the fudge into 8 x 8 rows, or 64 even pieces. Place each piece in a petit-four or mini muffin paper cup.
6. Enjoy immediately, or store in the refrigerator for up to 3 weeks in an airtight container, with wax paper in between each layer.

KAZAKHSTAN
IRAN
CHINA
INDIA
ARABIAN SEA
BAY OF BENGAL
SRI LANKA
SEYCHELLES
MAURITIUS
INDIAN OCEAN

7

The Best of Both Worlds

RUTH GYLLENHAMMER

The summer after I turned twenty-five, my husband and I moved across the world. I was accepted to a graduate program in China; my husband, David, took a new job in global business development. Together, we decided this was as good a time as any to bolster our résumés with international experience. In a matter of weeks, we sold almost all the contents of our one-bedroom apartment, entrusted the care of our two-year-old dog to my parents, and boarded a nonstop westbound flight, touching down fourteen hours later in Shanghai.

When we arrived at the bustling metropolitan airport, there was no one to pick us up. We made our own way, towing our oversized luggage and boarding the futuristic maglev train into the city. When we emerged, I felt like Dorothy waking up in the land of Oz. *We're not in California anymore.*

The English translations for the Chinese characters no longer appeared on the signage like they did at the airport. Instead of freeways filled with oversized SUVs, we saw bumper-to-bumper taxis, rickshaws, and bicycles. Everywhere we looked were skyscrapers, drawing our eyes upward to a sunless, smog-filled sky.

For the months and weeks leading up to that hot August day when we finally landed in Shanghai, I had only been looking forward. New city! New apartment! New food! New language! I imagined the person I would be in China—traveled and cosmopolitan, ambitious and brave. Yet as I breathed in the city air, sticky with humidity and sweat, all I could think about was what we had left behind: our friends, our family, the ocean breeze, even our holiday traditions. Another round-trip international flight was not in our immediate future; we wouldn't be back home for Christmas.

Suddenly, I was desperate for anything that bore a resemblance to the familiar. Instead of an apartment in a high-rise, we rented a standalone studio apartment with a courtyard in the heart of the former French Concession. The studio was nestled in a tree-lined cobblestone street reminiscent of Brooklyn or Paris. We had McDonald's McFlurries delivered to our door via Sherpa's, Shanghai delivery drivers who transported food in cooler bags on the backs of motorcycles years before DoorDash or Grubhub existed. My mother-in-law sent us monthly care packages of American snacks, mostly Cool Ranch Doritos, that we rationed for particularly acute moments of homesickness.

But we couldn't live off imported Doritos alone. I realized we had a choice: Keep wishing we were someplace else or be here—*really* here.

The exchange rate and lower cost of living worked in our favor, so David and I spent nights and weekends trying restaurants around town. At first, we gravitated to foreigner-friendly fare: smoothies and salmon pasta from Wagas and nachos from Shanghai Brewery. On a neighboring street, past a nail salon and cobbler, we found a restaurant combined with a specialty food store, not unlike the famed Joan's on Third in Los Angeles. Around the corner was a newly opened barbecue joint specializing in Texas-style brisket.

Day after day, we learned to choose expansiveness over comfort and adventure over isolation.

Through an online forum for expats, I found a blog called *Gourmet DIY Shanghai* that offered diverse recipes that could be replicated with local ingredients. I learned to make chicken tikka masala on my single-burner stovetop. When the Turkish restaurant opened down the street from our studio, we were the first diners. I, ever the interior design fanatic, appreciated the restaurant's high-end, all-plush velvet finishes and dim sconce lighting. In the center was a fireplace, and for fancy date nights during the cold Shanghai winters, we went there for warmth and for the delight of the hot Turkish tea they served in delicate glass mugs with snow-white sugar cubes.

Each new restaurant was an opportunity to notice the nuances of our environment. Over sushi, or wood-fired pizza, or the Shanghai take on Texas barbecue, we learned to slow down and lean into the shared, embodied experience of meals. Food became the physical means by which we connected with each other and with the city.

Weeks later, when we happened upon a noodle shop that felt less like a restaurant and more like a home kitchen, it felt like we had arrived. We were no longer lost tourists; we were settled expatriates. In other restaurants, we could pick out the foreigners based on their conversations, but here all we could hear was Shanghainese. When I stumbled through my poorly accented Mandarin to order, trying to quickly decipher the menu written solely in Chinese characters, the shop owner seemed to take pity on us and, without a word, brought us steaming bowls of pork-topped noodles. I still don't know how to order that exact dish, but to this day, they were the best noodles I've ever had.

They say that to really know a place, to be a good visitor, to truly experience a country's culture, you have to eat its food. So we kept eating.

We ate tea eggs and sesame buns from street vendors. At business dinners, my husband tried boiled intestines, sea cucumbers, and *mapo tofu*—classic Sichuan spicy tofu. We began venturing beyond our tourist-friendly neighborhood to the city outskirts and surrounding towns. We visited Nanxiang, the home of *xiao long bao*—soup dumplings. For my Chinese language teacher's wedding in Nanjing, we ate eight—an auspicious number in Chinese culture—courses of food, each with symbolic significance. Each experience expanded our palate.

By the time our first guests arrived—my college roommates—at the Lunar New Year in February, we were ready to show off our hard-won insider knowledge. We were so confident we could celebrate the holiday like locals that we bought our own fireworks to set off in the courtyard. One firework sparked early, and in the video I have, all you can see and hear are the sparks and loud bangs before my friend's terrified laugh-cry call out to David, "Are you okay?" (My husband, miraculously, still has all his fingers.) Not all our attempts to impress our friends backfired quite so spectacularly.

We took our visitors to the smoky Moroccan lounge on the water in People's Park, the Shanghai equivalent of Central Park. We took the subway to the walkable Xintiandi area of the city, where after shopping for souvenirs, we savored xiao long bao from the beloved Taiwanese restaurant chain Din Tai Fung. One of the best-kept secret happy hours was at the upscale Morton's steakhouse, so we rode the metro to the other side of the city, where we ate the unlimited steak sandwiches served alongside our green apple and chocolate "Mortinis."

Food became the way we experienced the city and the way we shared it, too. We couldn't offer a guest bedroom or a home-cooked meal, but we could tell our friends where to eat and how to get there.

When our family came to visit, the first place we took them was our favorite Italian restaurant, Bella Napoli, owned by an Italian and Belgian couple. We wanted to show them our favorite places, eateries with interesting culinary fusion, but food in China could be intimidating. Visiting a new place can generate fear of the unknown or anxiety about trying new things, so we started with cuisine a little more familiar, something a little closer to home. We began our night with beef carpaccio, the thin slices of raw beef melting in our mouths like butter, and with pasta, cooked perfectly al dente in a rich, red Bolognese.

Like we did when we were new to Shanghai, we explored from our neighborhood outward. Each expedition with our extended family became like a stepping stone—*try this new thing, then another, then another*. We traveled to the Great Wall of China, took an overnight train to Huangshan, and ventured to an off-the-beaten-path mountain town called Moganshan. We helped our visitors barter for custom-made trench coats and ate perfectly crispy Peking duck at the restaurant Da Dong. We ate more soup dumplings and more steaming bowls of pork noodles, and on the very last night, we sipped amaretto sours from a rooftop deck off The Bund amid the glow of the city lights and the shimmering water. Our hearts were full with friendship and food, and we didn't even have to cook.

Food became the way we experienced the city and the way we shared it, too.

In his book *Habits of the Household*, author Justin Whitmel Earley wrote, "In the story of God, eating is not just some daily routine of cramming food that allows us to survive, it is a ritual of communing with others that allows us to thrive. . . . Rarely is food just about physical nourishment; it is always about driving us toward relationship with God and others."[1]

That year in the city cemented this truth for us: Shared meals become shared memories. In Shanghai we established a pattern of fellowship, a habit of coming together around the table. This custom became woven into the underlying fabric of our family culture long before we moved back to Southern California, where our household grew to three, then four, then five, then six.

A meal is more than the sum of its parts, more than food and drinks and ambiance and company. A meal is the means to something greater. *Connection. Celebration. Communion.*

Food was medicine to us, not in the way it healed our bodies, but in how the meals around a new city—shared with each other, with family, and with friends—became a balm to our souls, a kind of antidote to homesickness. The food of a new city combined with the company of home? That was the best of both worlds.

Food was medicine to us, not in the way it healed our bodies, but in how the meals around a new city became a balm to our souls, a kind of antidote to homesickness.

Chicken Tikka Masala

I've adapted this recipe from Gourmet DIY Shanghai*—a blog from a fellow Shanghai expatriate I followed during the season I lived in Shanghai.*[2] *This is a great weeknight meal that comes together with minimal effort. While the chicken marinates, I like to "pregame" dinner with a starter of veggies. Baby carrots and sliced cucumbers with hummus are the current fan favorite.*

MAKES ABOUT 4 ENTRÉE SERVINGS

For the marinade

1 cup plain yogurt
1 tablespoon lemon juice
1 tablespoon fresh ginger, minced (about 1-inch knob of ginger)
2 teaspoons ground cumin
1 teaspoon ground cinnamon
1 teaspoon paprika
1 heaping teaspoon kosher salt
1/4 teaspoon black pepper
1/4 teaspoon cayenne pepper
1 pound chicken breasts or thighs, cut into 1-inch cubes

For the marinade

1. In a medium bowl or zip-top bag, mix the yogurt, lemon juice, ginger, cumin, cinnamon, paprika, salt, black pepper, and cayenne pepper.
2. Add the chicken and stir until coated with the yogurt marinade.
3. Move the chicken to the refrigerator and marinate for 30 minutes to an hour.

For the sauce

2 teaspoons ground cumin

2 teaspoons paprika

1 teaspoon kosher salt

2 tablespoons butter

2 cloves garlic, minced

1 (6-ounce) can tomato paste

3/4 cup water

1/2 teaspoon granulated sugar

1 cup heavy cream

1/4 cup cilantro, chopped, for garnish, optional

For the sauce

1. In a small bowl, combine the cumin, paprika, and salt then set aside.
2. In a Dutch oven or large skillet, melt the butter over medium heat. Add the garlic and sauté until fragrant, about 1 minute.
3. Add the bowl of cumin, paprika, and salt to the butter and garlic, and cook until the spices are fragrant and toasted, about 1 more minute. Stir in the tomato paste and cook for another minute, then add the water and the sugar. Stir until smooth, then add the heavy cream.
4. When all the sauce ingredients are fully incorporated, add the chicken-yogurt mixture to the pan. Cook for 10 minutes over medium heat, stirring occasionally, until the chicken is thoroughly cooked and the sauce has thickened slightly.
5. Serve over rice and top with chopped cilantro, if using. A side of warm garlic naan is a great way to sop up the sauce!

Note: For the yogurt, I prefer to use plain Greek yogurt. And instead of table salt, I use Diamond Crystal kosher salt, which has larger flakes.

8

You Never Quite Forget

NEIDY HESS

My husband, Zach, and I step off our flight from Omaha to New Orleans, full of excitement to be away for once. I try not to text Amanda because I don't want to shift her focus—she gets married in less than a day. But she beats me to it anyway.

If you're hungry after your flight, stop by Killer PoBoys! Amanda exclaims via text. I wanted to reply back, *Forget about me! I'm fine!* But there she was again, ready with a recommendation and an invitation.

Even after arranging childcare with grandparents, Zach swapping shifts with another firefighter, and me using my paid time off, the math wasn't mathing—our budget was tight. It took a miracle to get us here.

Still, my best friend from high school wanted me to attend her wedding. How could I miss it?

PoBoys sounds AMAZING! I text back.

Another text bubble popped up. *And don't forget about the beignets! You need those, too!*

Trust me. I won't forget those either.

"Today, we're doing a group activity," our AP English teacher informed us. My jaw dropped so fast that the hinges of my skull ached. I protest in my mind. *English is a solitary activity—essay writing is supposed to be done alone.* My teacher, who was certainly alive when Charlotte Brontë wrote *Jane Eyre*, pointed to me and then two other students with her bony finger, Grim Reaper–style.

Time of my death: 3:15 p.m., Wednesday, September 27, 2006.

The other two students scooted closer to my desk. I begrudgingly said hello. Amanda, one of the two students, introduced herself. We talked about the project briefly, then the bell rang.

I didn't think Amanda was serious about our AP English project since she was known to goof around in class, but she continued to prod after school. She drove to my apartment to convince my strict, unflinching Mexican mother to let me work on a school project with her in a public space away from my mother's supervision. Somehow my mother cracked—Amanda was allowed to drive me to her house.

"We have to make a stop first!" she shouted once I was in the car. I gasped, thinking my mother would notice that we'd deviated from the plan we'd cleared with her, but no one could convince Amanda to let go of an adventure. She drove a few minutes down one of the busiest roads in Atlanta and parked her car at Publix, a grocery store by her house. I placed my hands in my pockets and followed her into the store.

Amanda meandered through the aisles and tried to decide what she wanted. But eventually we ended up at the deli counter.

"Have you had their shaved ham? You have to try it!" Amanda exclaimed. Her earnest enthusiasm caught me off guard, so I laughed. I took a bite of her sample and smiled.

"Amanda—you're not kidding! This is pretty bomb!"

She nodded. "See? I told you!" She grabbed her package of ham from the butcher. She also took two chocolate milk bottles off the shelf, one for me and another for her. We left and drove to her house.

We turned up the volume on the car radio, sang along to Britney Spears, and laughed some more. Then she turned the volume down during a commercial.

"How long have you lived here?" I asked. I didn't see her much the year before—our friend groups must have been different.

Amanda, full of giggles and song lyrics, grew serious. Her face froze for a moment.

"Well, I moved here almost a year ago. I used to go to a private school in New Orleans, but . . . Katrina changed that."

My heart sank into my stomach.

For the next few minutes, she told me about losing everything in the hurricane—how she missed her old friends and her school uniform. Oh, and the beignets! She missed grabbing those with her mom on the weekends. Beignets, the more dressed-up version of a donut and the aristocratic cousin to the funnel cake, were her favorite. Cafe Du Monde had the best ones, but she loved the ones from Cafe Beignet, too. She told me about the music, the parties at Mardi Gras, and all the beauty from her old home.

"I'm sorry," I whispered.

She sighed and then smiled. "It's okay. I'm here now!" She parked and we hopped out. We cemented our friendship at that moment—doing schoolwork with shaved ham and bottled chocolate milk.

The light poured into my maid of honor's living room—a picture-perfect landscape for my wedding day preparation. Only I was upset. The day wasn't what I had pictured. I overheard a comment in the other room: "She shouldn't have paired raspberry, navy, *and* red. It's too much."

Humiliation bloomed on my cheeks, accompanying my bright-red lipstick and the cat-eyeliner. The comment made me second-guess all my wedding choices. Today didn't feel like mine.

Standing on the other side of the room, Amanda smoothed out her navy blue bridesmaid dress. She noticed my disposition as I struggled to put on my wedding dress.

"I got you," Amanda encouraged. She painstakingly buttoned each button on the back of my dress and figured out how to attach my bustle so she could affix the train later. The photographer smiled and took our photo. I blushed.

"I didn't see that coming! Sorry," I apologized.

Amanda giggled. But she didn't know I was sorry for more than just the candid shot; I regretted not asking her to be my maid of honor in place of someone else. Amanda, who came into town regardless of how much it cost her, was here. She wasn't just a ghost from my past—she was present.

"You look beautiful. This all does," she said as she smoothed out the bottom part of my dress.

The corners of my mouth curled up, but tears pooled around my eyelashes.

"Thank you for being here," I whispered.

"I wouldn't miss it," she said.

After our wedding, Zach and I moved to San Diego, where I got caught up in the daily projects of being a young wife and mom. Amanda became busy with work after college. Nothing spectacular closed the chapter of our high school friendship; it just quietly fizzled out. We simply vanished from one another's lives.

Still, we tried to make our friendship work. When my eldest, Charlie, was born, Amanda gave him a stuffed lamb, which he played with through his toddler years. I thought of her whenever I watched him carry around his little lamb. I sent infrequent texts, and she sent me pictures of the exciting places she visited. I followed her on social media, where I saw pictures of her wild party days while I cradled my new baby. But our attempts weren't enough to keep our communication and friendship alive.

After months of no communication, she sent me a text update about a man she was dating. I squealed. I daydreamed of her future wedding to this potential match. But then we went months without talking again.

One night, after I put Charlie to bed with his stuffed lamb, I felt a nudge to text her. *She wouldn't want to hear from me. Who wants to hear from the toddler mom?* I thought. But I listened to the inkling and sent the text anyway.

Can I call you? she texted back. Charlie began to squirm. *He'll be okay*, I thought. I texted back, *Absolutely.*

After an awkward hello over the phone, I heard her take a deep breath. She then detailed the heartbreak she'd experienced over the past year. She'd broken up with her boyfriend. It was a terrible ending. Even with our distance in different cities and seasons, it was like we were sitting in the Publix parking lot talking about New Orleans. Once again, I held her grief, because no

Once again, I held her grief, because no matter how much time had passed or how much had changed in our lives, my friend knew I couldn't forget her.

matter how much time had passed or how much had changed in our lives, my friend knew I couldn't forget her.

I had almost let go of a friend who was there for me during my most challenging years of growing up—just because of circumstances. I made every excuse not to keep our relationship going. *My life is far too dull for her—I have a toddler. I'm knee-deep in twenty-piece puzzles, preschool songs, and potty training. We're in different seasons. I'm just a ghost of her past.*

But the truth is, even when life, schedules, and distance keep us apart from our kindred spirits, we never forget what it's like to *just* be friends. Our shared histories bind us together because our histories haunt our grown selves in the best way possible.

On the phone with Amanda, I broke our silence. "I got you," I said, making a promise.

Amanda sniffled, not saying a word.

I added, "I'll also be there when you get married. It'll be in New Orleans, right? Because I've never been."

The first time Amanda told me about beignets, she'd described them as "fried, sweet heaven." And now I can smell them outside my hotel door.

The sweet smell of fried, pillowy dough traces along the French Quarter alleys lined with cafés, the aroma she had said would woo me. But you wouldn't want to go down the wrong alley—Amanda also warned me about the awful biohazard smell down certain passageways. Still, I can't wait to meet my friend's memory of a sweet pastry and a warm café au lait. What a way to celebrate an incredible milestone in her life.

On the day of Amanda's wedding, Zach and I wander in and out of art galleries, trinket shops, and antique shops. We gawk at musicians on the streets. We get caught in torrential rain, hoping the fat drops will dissipate before the wedding later that afternoon. I feel like we're walking around in Amanda's favorite memories from her time growing up in New Orleans.

And then it's time. We run back to our hotel to get dressed and prepare for an evening full of festivities—beignets and all. My husband buttons the back of my dress, and I buckle my strappy heels, which I know might be a mistake on the cobbled ground. Thankfully, a bike taxi waits outside our hotel's large open doors. I nod to the bellhop, who's dressed in a maroon uniform. He opens my door.

The museum that hosts Amanda's wedding features gruesome stories of medical treatments gone awry and even displays a haunting set of medical tools and medications—ghost stories of what once was. For someone as sunshiny as Amanda, the irony tickles me. But I love that she's the type of person to pair macabre history with the delight of her wedding day.

For the next hour, I witness my friend marry a man who knows her stories, sorrows, and joys. I watch her hold an umbrella while a tuba, euphonium, and trumpets blare a wedding song down the streets. The French Quarter cobblestones hold us as we yell, "*Laissez les bons temps rouler!* Let the good times roll!"

Amanda's wedding is everything I daydreamed it would be in our teen years. I never want to forget it. We still belong in each other's worlds regardless of how much we think we've grown apart. I'm glad I stopped thinking about the busyness of life to remember my friend. That moment I decided to reach out to her is as sweet as the beignets.

For the rest of the evening, we sing songs at the top of our lungs. We hoot and holler in the street, even as a funeral band passes. In New Orleans, you can't tell the difference between the funeral and wedding songs—and still, we dance.

Bite-Size Lemon Beignets

Just like an old friendship takes time and space to grow, these beignets require a lot of waiting and even a time for separation. And after all your work, the sweet, tangy flavor shines through the puffy pastry. Inspired from an old Creole recipe and Cafe Du Monde's beignets recipe, make sure not to skimp out on the powdered sugar in each bite!

MAKES 2 TO 3 DOZEN BEIGNETS

1/2 cup water, warmed to 105 to 110 degrees
1/4 cup lemon juice, warmed to 105 to 110 degrees
1 1/4 teaspoons quick-rising yeast
1/3 cup granulated sugar
2 eggs, whites and yolks separated
1/2 cup whole milk
1 teaspoon vanilla
3 1/2 cups all-purpose flour
Grated zest of 2 lemons
1/2 teaspoon salt
Vegetable oil for frying
Juice of 1 lemon for garnish
Powdered sugar for garnish

1. In a small bowl, combine the water, lemon juice, yeast, and sugar. Let the mixture sit for about 15 minutes, until the yeast dissolves and begins to froth. Set aside.
2. While the yeast is frothing, in a medium bowl, whisk the egg yolks, milk, and vanilla together until frothy. Set aside.
3. In another medium bowl, mix the flour, lemon zest, and salt.
4. In a stand mixer or with a hand mixer fitted with a whisk attachment, beat egg whites until they are stiff, about 4 minutes. Add the yolk mixture and continue mixing for 30 seconds. Stop the mixer and add the flour and lemon zest mixture. Remove the whisk attachment from the mixer and fit the mixer with a dough hook. Mix the dough until it pulls away from the bowl, about 3 to 4 minutes. Be careful not to overmix!

5. Flour your hands and remove the dough from the mixer. Gently roll the dough into a ball, and place the dough ball into a large bowl to rise. Cover with plastic wrap and a towel, and leave the dough to rise for 1½ hours.
6. Lightly flour the counter or a hard surface, and roll the dough to ⅛-inch thickness. Keep extra flour on hand to apply to the top of the dough to keep the dough from sticking to the rolling pin. Cut into 1½-inch squares.
7. Prepare your frying station: On the counter near the stove, line a cookie sheet with paper towels. Pour 2 inches of oil in a large pot, preferably a 6-quart Dutch oven or larger, and heat to 370 degrees. Once the oil reaches frying temperature, add one square of dough to the oil to test the frying conditions. Once one side of the dough is puffy and golden, about 1 to 2 minutes, flip the dough to fry on the other side. When both sides are golden and puffy, remove the beignet from the oil and place it on the prepared cookie sheet. Continue frying, adding a single layer of beignets to the pan, about 6 to 7 beignets. Always make sure to maintain 2 inches of frying oil at 370 degrees.
8. Once you're done frying your beignets, sprinkle each with fresh lemon juice, followed by generous amounts of powdered sugar through a sieve. Serve immediately.

Note: You can make beignets without serving immediately. Store in an airtight container for up to one day. For best results, don't add lemon juice and powdered sugar until ready to eat.

9

A Burden Split Three Ways

CARA STOLEN

The door to my friend's in-home salon creaks a little as I struggle to open it around an armload of cloth grocery bags. Kay Cee rushes across the finished concrete floor, takes the bags from me, and lays them at the foot of the facial table in the middle of the room. My arms now free, I give her a quick, tight hug.

"How are you?" she asks. "I can't believe we're doing this!"

"I know!" I squeal.

Just then, our other friend, Celeste, stumbles through the door in similar fashion, and Kay Cee and I hurry to unburden her. We exchange hugs, then stand in a collective pause, surveying the mountain of backpacking gear in front of us.

Though I grew up backpacking with my parents and used to plan trips with my husband, Levi, all the time, it's been nine years since my last trip. Standing here, looking at our old four-season tent and other gear laid out in front of me, I can't help but remember some of the incredible trips Levi and I have taken together as a couple. The seven-day loop with perfect weather in September. The weekend trips to our favorite lakes. The trip we took when I was pregnant with our firstborn, Royce.

All these sweet memories are a stark contrast to the disaster of a day we'd spent in the mountains a few weeks ago—a day I'd begged him to spend with me, only to come home feeling more disconnected than ever.

I shake the thought away almost unconsciously, my coping mechanisms taking over. Those feelings of sadness and longing get stuffed back where they belong: out of sight. With the most backpacking experience in this group, I feel a sense of responsibility that our upcoming trip goes smoothly. And nobody needs a leader in the midst of a crisis. I'm excited for this trip, and that's all anyone needs to know right now.

I can't remember who suggested a backpacking trip. It may have been me—I'm the connecting link in this trio—but the idea could have belonged just as easily to Kay Cee or Celeste. What I *do* remember is how the spark of an idea grew into a full-fledged plan. On a group text we started after a snowshoe hike a few years ago, we proposed dates and suggested trail ideas. I sent out potential itineraries and put together gear lists. Finally, we landed on a forty-mile loop in Washington's Goat Rocks Wilderness that we'd take four days and three nights in July to complete.

I've hiked countless miles with Kay Cee and have climbed numerous peaks with Celeste, but the three of us have only hiked together a handful of times. Four days on trail together might seem a little insane, except somehow it doesn't at all. Sometimes, with friendship, you just know.

My thoughts are interrupted by Celeste asking if she should start weighing out gear on the kitchen scale she brought. Kay Cee grabs a pad of paper and a pen, and I start digging through the gear.

"Should we split up the tent?" Kay Cee asks, taking the tent out of its stuff sack.

I watch her hand Celeste the poles, then the stakes, then the tent separately. Though we'd discussed at length taking only one tent, it never occurred to me that we might split up the components. I'd assumed I alone would have to carry everything I needed.

Once the gear is weighed, we lay out oatmeal packets, instant coffee, and tuna pouches on the facial table. I coach them through putting together three nights' worth of dinners from old *Backpacker* magazine recipes I still have memorized. Then we consult the list of weights Celeste compiled and split it all out evenly between us. I take Saturday's food, the tent poles, an ultralight pot, and a fuel canister, then marvel at how light the gear feels split three ways.

It's still dark the morning of our trip—a sign of just *how* early it is when the sun already rises at 5:15 a.m. I shower, get dressed, and haul my pack to the car, then come back to say goodbye to Levi. He'd seemed ambivalent when I broached the idea of this trip, unbothered by the idea of my absence. But this morning, he pulls me in for a long, sleepy hug and responds to my "I love you" with a whispered "I love you, too." I pull out of the driveway and try to remember the last time he said those three words.

I stuff those feelings away, too.

The three of us meet at Kay Cee's house again and chat the entire three-hour drive to the trailhead. Kay Cee tells us how farming is going this year and how weird it is that her sons are gone for a week with her parents. Celeste talks about her new puppy and tries to explain how her new private practice job works. We talk about saying goodbye to our husbands and joke about whether or not they'll survive without us. To most people, I imagine, it would be the perfect segue to open up about marital struggles, but I'm not even sure I know how.

We leave the trailhead around 8:30 a.m. and immediately climb the steep incline up Nanny Ridge. My pack, which felt so manageable when we split up the gear, seems to grow heavier with every step. Less than a mile up the trail, sweat pours down my face and back, and we stop to shed our long sleeves and pull our hair back. My friends laugh about the weight of their packs and being out of shape, but I soldier on, unwilling to show weakness or complain. *I've done harder things.*

An hour later, when the trail levels out and we get our first glimpse of Mount Adams, I forget all about my heavy pack, overwhelmed by the specific awe and wonder I feel in the presence of mountains. It doesn't matter if I'm standing at a vantage point with a view or actually standing on top of the mountain—either way, the feeling is the same. It's an overwhelming sense of how small I am in the grand scheme of creation, a tiny speck in the midst of all this wonder—*and* a feeling of strength and power within myself. It's a feeling that takes over my entire body and spirit. It's the only time I'm ever completely calm.

It's an overwhelming sense of how small I am in the grand scheme of creation, a tiny speck in the midst of all this wonder.

Standing here with my two friends, on a small rocky outcropping just below the trail, I'm shocked to find I can still feel awe. The only thing I've felt for months is agonizing sadness over my crumbling marriage, and the relief of feeling wonder—of feeling anything besides despair—is so intense that it brings tears to my eyes. I'm grateful for the cover of my sunglasses.

Midmorning, we stop at a lake for lunch, then traipse across wildflower-covered hillsides before climbing up a pass to Cispus Basin, where we set up camp for the night. As luck would have it, the perfect campsite is open—tucked behind a few trees above the trail, the spring-fed headwaters of the Cispus River next to it, craggy peaks everywhere I look.

While Kay Cee takes a nap in the tent, Celeste and I walk over to the stream and take off our boots to soak our sore feet in the frigid rushing water. For the first time in a long time, I feel calm and at peace, with mountains and wildflowers everywhere I look. And something within me breaks loose. Looking south across the Washington Cascades, I find myself asking Celeste, a licensed mental health counselor, if she can recommend a therapist at her practice. In her calm, kind therapist tone—the same one she's used to talk me across rock ledges, over sheer drop-offs, and up climbing walls—she asks follow-up questions, while somehow still letting me lead. I didn't mean to tell her any of it. I meant to keep these feelings all bottled up inside—meant to keep pretending to the world and my friends (and myself) that I have it all together—but as the conversation goes on, I tell her I haven't been sleeping much. That Levi and I aren't doing well. That my marriage is in some sort of tortuous holding pattern where Levi and I are both hurt and disconnected.

I tell her I'm not sure we'll make it.

And she listens. *Really* listens. She nods. She affirms. I've been so afraid that saying everything out loud would somehow make it more real. Or that opening up to someone would be a betrayal of Levi and our relationship. Or that whomever I told would do that well-meaning thing where they try to side with you, and I would end up feeling like they thought less of the man I love.

But as we walk back up to the tent, I don't feel any of those things. Instead, I feel seen. Understood. I feel just the tiniest bit lighter and drift off to sleep easily for the first night in I can't remember how long.

In the morning, before we leave camp, we reshuffle our remaining food supply for the trip to lighten everyone's load equally. But when we set off down the trail again, it's not just my pack weight that feels more manageable. That bag of feelings I've been carrying around feels less weighty, too. I'm fully present. I laugh more.

We make camp that afternoon above a waterfall, Mount Rainier towering above us. Tired and at ease with each other after two days on trail, we settle into the meadow with playing cards and snacks.

I knew that backpacking together would put the accelerator on our friendship, but I'm surprised by the intimacy of it all. We've taken bites of each other's food and drunk off each other's water bladder hoses. We've shared a tent after a day of hiking and no showers. We've talked about our menstrual cycles and used the bathroom in each other's vicinity. At this point in the trip, I'm closer to Kay Cee and Celeste than I've been to anyone since my childhood best friend. We've become trail sisters.

I have a history of opening up in friendship, only to push that same friend away, terrified of the closeness my vulnerability has created. I keep everyone at arm's length, afraid of what could happen if I let them see the cracks in my exterior. But today, as the conversation flows, instead of shutting down and pushing Celeste away, I find myself building on the momentum of the night before. I tell them stories of backpacking with Levi and talk about how much I miss him—not lack-of-proximity missing, but a deep, devastating longing for my partner and friend, who sometimes feels so distant that I'm afraid we'll never close the gap again.

We lay it all out in the open: hard marriages, financial strain, parenting fatigue, career uncertainty. With an open expanse of time, without places to be or tasks to complete or anything to distract ourselves with, nothing is off limits. We share pieces of ourselves and swipe at tears and laugh until the tears fall again. Then we snuggle up in our sleeping bags and fall asleep looking at the mountain, all our loads a little lighter.

When I pull back in the driveway after our trip, everything will not miraculously be better. Yet somehow, the weight of it all will be tolerable. Made so by the balm of the mountains, yes. But more so by friendship and the willingness of those friends to help me carry my burdens.

Everything but the Kitchen Sink Trail Mix

There are two things I look forward to on every hiking trip: the views and the snacks. And the longer the trip is, the more the snack part of the equation matters. Something my friends and I love to do is to bring each other trail treats—extra little goodies to make a summit or a rest stop a bit sweeter. Think of this recipe as a jumping-off point; add more of what you like and ditch what you don't.

MAKES 6 SERVINGS

3/4 cup sprouted almonds, roasted almonds, or sliced almonds
1/2 cup hazelnuts, or any other nut you fancy
1/2 cup golden raisins
1/2 cup dried cranberries
1/2 cup dark chocolate chips, mini peanut butter cups, or M&M's
3/4 cup peanut butter–filled pretzels or regular pretzels
1 1/2 cups cinnamon crunch cereal or granola clusters

1. In a large bowl, mix together the almonds, hazelnuts, golden raisins, dried cranberries, chocolate, pretzels, and cereal.
2. Scoop 3/4 cup of the mix into zip-top bags, then hit the trail!

10

When Friendships Change

SONYA SPILLMANN

Walking around the park one day, I noticed a mother I'd never seen before. She was tall and pretty, fair-skinned with dark hair, and dressed nicely in business clothes—a stark contrast to my comfortable pants and oversized shirt. She pushed the handle of a tricycle on which her daughter, who looked like a life-size doll, rode with wide eyes. We approached each other, exchanged smiles, and went on our way.

My days at the time were made of the same enjoyable but repetitive routine: Make breakfast, play with my daughter, head to the park down the block or attempt a local outing, and make sure to be home before naptime. Afterward, back to the park for a quick walk with the dog, then home again to make dinner. It was during those afternoon walks when I started to notice the other mom. She was always in business clothes, sometimes taking calls, usually with her daughter on a push tricycle. In time, our smiles turned into audible hellos.

Then one day we stopped long enough to exchange the small talk mothers do: "She's so cute! How old?" Then another day: "What's her name? So pretty." And another: "What's your name? Live close by?"

The next time we saw each other, we slowed to say hello, and both

As our bellies grew, so did the seed of a deeply meaningful friendship.

girls squirmed to be unstrapped. The other mother and I stood there, making pleasant conversation, while our kids ran around, squealing and laughing and free. I don't remember who said what, but we likely reintroduced ourselves—her name was Heather—and continued to talk. As our casual interactions grew more frequent, Heather disclosed to me that she was pregnant again. I was, too. We were due four months apart.

As our bellies grew, so did the seed of a deeply meaningful friendship.

After our sons were born, our paths continued to cross. She extended her maternity leave and eventually quit her job. We'd run into each other at the coffee shop and, if we had time, sit down on the same couch while the girls drank juice boxes and destroyed their muffins. It didn't take long to realize just how similar our personalities were—we both wore our hearts on our sleeves, couldn't bother with details, felt knocked over by motherhood but also loved it. We were avid readers, didn't measure ingredients when we cooked, and couldn't follow a recipe to save our lives. We preferred challenging conversations over small talk, we each had a parent pass away, and neither of us lived near our immediate family—though she had cousins close by and a large network of friends from her years of working in the city.

Our park and coffee shop meetups turned into toddler park playdates, which eventually led to living-room hangouts and outings all around DC. We'd strap our kids into car seats and drive to the country to pick berries, or out to a local farm to see baby pigs, or into the city where our two- and four-year-olds would run around the National Museum of Natural History, explore the hands-on area at the National Air and Space Museum, and laugh at the llamas during our many trips to the zoo.

To know Heather was to understand that her door—and table—were always open. *Yes! Stop by! Come in! Sit down!* There was always room for one more. Always more food. *And her food.* I liked to cook, in the sense that I liked eating and generally enjoyed being creative in the kitchen. I'd devoured Anthony Bourdain's memoir, *Kitchen Confidential*, owned one expensive knife, and thought that keeping six different types of vinegar on hand was normal. I asked for cookbooks for Christmas and had taught myself to make baklava, crème brûlée, and molten chocolate lava cakes. But even in this, I didn't really understand that there was a difference between cooking and baking.

But Heather did. And she was a cook. She understood flavor combinations and temperature levels and which measurements were just suggestions and which weren't. She was more than just brave and daring; she had *instinct.* She knew how much acidity something needed, how to balance that acid with sweetness. And everything she made, and I mean *everything*—salmon, chicken, burgers, even egg salad and asparagus—was elevated to something you'd take a bite of and just shake your head at in disbelief and pleasure. Her salsa—an irreproducible combination of tomatoes, cilantro, garlic, lime juice, vinegar, and salt—was so good that people would joke about drinking it. Her tacos? Each tortilla, filled with perfectly seasoned beef, was placed into a cast-iron skillet, and she'd stand there and fry until an entire baking tray was full. Then she'd offer us, her friends, as many tacos as we could eat. And then there was her brisket. It melted, I mean *melted*, in your mouth while also cascading an explosion of flavors across the surface of your tongue. You'd barely chew, and it would drip with reminders of everything you found comforting in life—friends, a soft blanket, a warm hug, a kiss on the cheek. *How is this possible?* I'd always wonder. *How is this so good?*

Heather introduced me to food writers Mark Bittman and Michael Pollan. And she was the first person I knew who took the concept of farm-to-table eating seriously. One Thanksgiving, she made a turkey—crisscrossed with bacon and decorated with oranges—that was raised only a couple of hours away from us. It was under her influence that I began to get weekly deliveries to my door of locally sourced fresh produce. Because of her, I felt confident enough to make mussels, roast a chicken each week (then make broth with the bones), and attempt an eggplant, roasted red pepper, and mozzarella terrine just because I wanted to. She was a generous friend with her recipes, her home, and her heart.

In the afternoon, we'd often put the boys down for a nap—her son in his room, mine in a Pack 'n Play—while the girls played together. We'd hang out until I'd reluctantly head home or she'd get started on dinner. And if we kept talking, she'd often say, "Just stay." I'd text my husband, *Dinner over here tonight*, then I'd get to work snapping green beans, or chopping garlic, or tossing potatoes in more olive oil, salt, and pepper than you'd think was necessary.

Heather's uncle had a house a few hours away, along a river in the Virginia countryside. One year for Memorial Day, she and her husband invited us to join her and her cousin's families there for the weekend. The kids fished, rode bikes, and played soccer on the front lawn. Our dogs ran wild, and the kids caught fireflies at dusk. We kayaked and canoed, and after making chicken nuggets for the little ones and getting them settled in for the night, we ate boiled crabs and drank beers and started a running joke about all the possible food combinations one could make with Old Bay. They invited us again the next year, and with that, Memorial Day at the country house became our little tradition.

One year, it was just our two families there the first night. Heather and I were cleaning up after dinner—me at the sink, her with a dish towel drying. What prompted us to talk about what happens after we die, I don't know. But the stakes of this conversation were real—this was no theoretical discussion. Nor was it the first time we'd talked about death, my Christian faith, her Jewish one, or our views on the meaning of life. But as mothers often are, we were interrupted and spent the rest of the evening putting kids to bed. Later, we swapped old stories through laughter, sitting in the living room with our husbands. It must have been close to midnight when the guys said good night, but she and I poured another glass of wine and kept on talking. Eventually, though, it was time to turn off the lights, check the doors, and get ourselves to bed.

In my memory, the conversation happened like this: "Look outside," one of us whispered at the front door. "Look at the stars." Then whether we said it out loud or simply thought it at the same time, I don't know: *Want to?* We didn't care that it was late; smiles crossed both our faces.

The longer we stared up into the heavens, the quieter we became.

We snuck into our bedrooms, grabbed blankets and socks, then tiptoed out the front door into the cool summer night air. We pulled two camp chairs over from the garage, sat down, and looked up. East to west, north to south, an expansive black sky bloomed in layers of light. In the quiet of the dark, we continued to talk, picking up our conversation from earlier. But the longer we stared up into the heavens, the quieter we became. Even the two of us, who rarely lacked for words, eventually fell silent. With more and more starlight arriving against the dark never-endingness, I began to feel very small. And I think she did, too.

One of us said something like, "Makes you wonder what we're here for." And the other, "How is it possible that we exist?"

Yet there we were. Two friends. With husbands and children sleeping in the house right behind us. Surreal. Holy. Wrapped in blankets, staring into eternity unfolding.

"What time is it?" my husband asked when I eventually crawled into bed. It was close to three, but I didn't want to tell him—the kids would be up in just a few hours. "What were you doing?" he asked next.

How could I tell him the truth? How could I *explain* the truth? That we just kept talking, until we didn't need to anymore. That it didn't seem like that much time had passed. That all those stars under such a big sky, contemplating loss and love and life, were so unexpectedly special, almost supernatural, that I didn't want it to end.

Instead, I laid my head down, closed my eyes, and simply said, "We were stargazing."

My family went to the country house for another year or two, but soon we moved out of the neighborhood, and later Heather and her family did, too. Our annual Memorial Day trips became fond memories, and even though Heather and I still saw each other, our visits became less and less frequent. Our families grew and the kids started school, and with all those changes, my time no longer felt like it was truly mine.

We'd still text. We'd occasionally talk. But our friendship was changing.

Is it fair to say that we were, too?

When friendships drift apart, it's tempting to look back and wonder: *Was it this? Was it that?* It's almost as if we're sticking a finger into water, trying to pin down something solid. And I believe it's too easy, too common, too obvious to fixate on the negative, on the lack, on what we once had but now don't anymore.

Are we putting on rose-colored glasses when we accept that some friendships, even deeply meaningful ones, may end up only being for a season? Is it possible to look back on that time and, instead of wondering about the turning point, simply appreciate how special that period was for as long as we had it?

We are the people we are today because of those friendships—even if those friendships are not the same today.

We are the people we are today because of those friendships—even if those friendships are not the same today. I was made from each playdate, each outing, every shared laugh, every witnessed tear. I am who I am because of all that time at the park, in the living room, in the kitchen, around a table. Every conversation, every memory, every recipe still used, all of it—*all of it*—is so, so dear.

I'm going to make your brisket for Christmas dinner, I texted Heather recently.

I still make your mom's apple cake every year for Rosh Hashanah, she texted back.

In a season of motherhood, when life could have been so hard, this friendship was—and always will be—a gift.

Heather's Brisket

Despite being an avid and even adventurous cook, I have never been confident in my ability to make large (and often expensive) cuts of meat. Which is why I love this recipe so much. It's easy, impressive, and jaw-droppingly delicious. The biggest commitment involves giving the brisket enough time to cook. I usually serve this during the holidays, but it can work any time of year. I'm forever grateful that Heather shared this recipe with me—and that she generously agreed that it could also be shared with you.

MAKES 4 TO 6 SERVINGS

1 4-pound beef brisket
2 tablespoons chili powder
2 tablespoons salt (yes, tablespoons)
1 tablespoon garlic powder
1 tablespoon onion powder
1 tablespoon ground black pepper
1 tablespoon granulated sugar
2 teaspoons dry mustard
1 bay leaf, crushed
1½ cups beef broth

1. Remove the brisket from the refrigerator about an hour before you plan to put it in the oven. (You want to remove the chill.)
2. Preheat the oven to 350 degrees. In a small bowl, combine the chili powder, salt, garlic powder, onion powder, black pepper, sugar, dry mustard, and bay leaf. Trim any excess fat off the sides of the brisket but not the top (the fat cap, or top layer of fat, adds flavor and tenderness).
3. Rub the trimmed brisket all over with the dry rub, leaving a thick layer of spices on top. Place the brisket in a roasting pan with the fat side up. Roast, uncovered, for 1 hour.
4. After an hour, lower the oven temperature to 300 degrees. Remove the pan from the oven, and pour in the beef broth around the meat so as not to disturb the rub. Then

carefully cover the pan tightly with foil and, if available, place the lid of the roasting pan on top.

5. Slide the pan back into the oven. Cook for 3 hours, for a total of approximately 1 hour per pound, until the meat shreds with zero effort. Slice the brisket against the grain into thin strips. Serve hot.

Notes: Water, vegetable broth, red wine, or whiskey can be subsituted or combined with the beef broth. My preference is 1 cup beef broth, 1/4 cup water, 1/4 cup whiskey.

If I'm cooking brisket during the holidays to serve a crowd, I start the night before. I use an 8-pound brisket, double the spices, and start cooking it around 10:00 p.m. at 350 degrees for 1 hour. Then at 11:00 p.m., I turn down the temperature to 300 degrees so the brisket can cook slowly throughout the night. In the morning, I wake up early to begin checking for doneness. When the meat is fork-tender, I pull it out and let it cool on the stovetop. Later in the day, I slice it and then reheat it in the oven. I love to serve this with roasted brussels sprouts, red wine, and nice bread to sop up the juices. Enjoy!

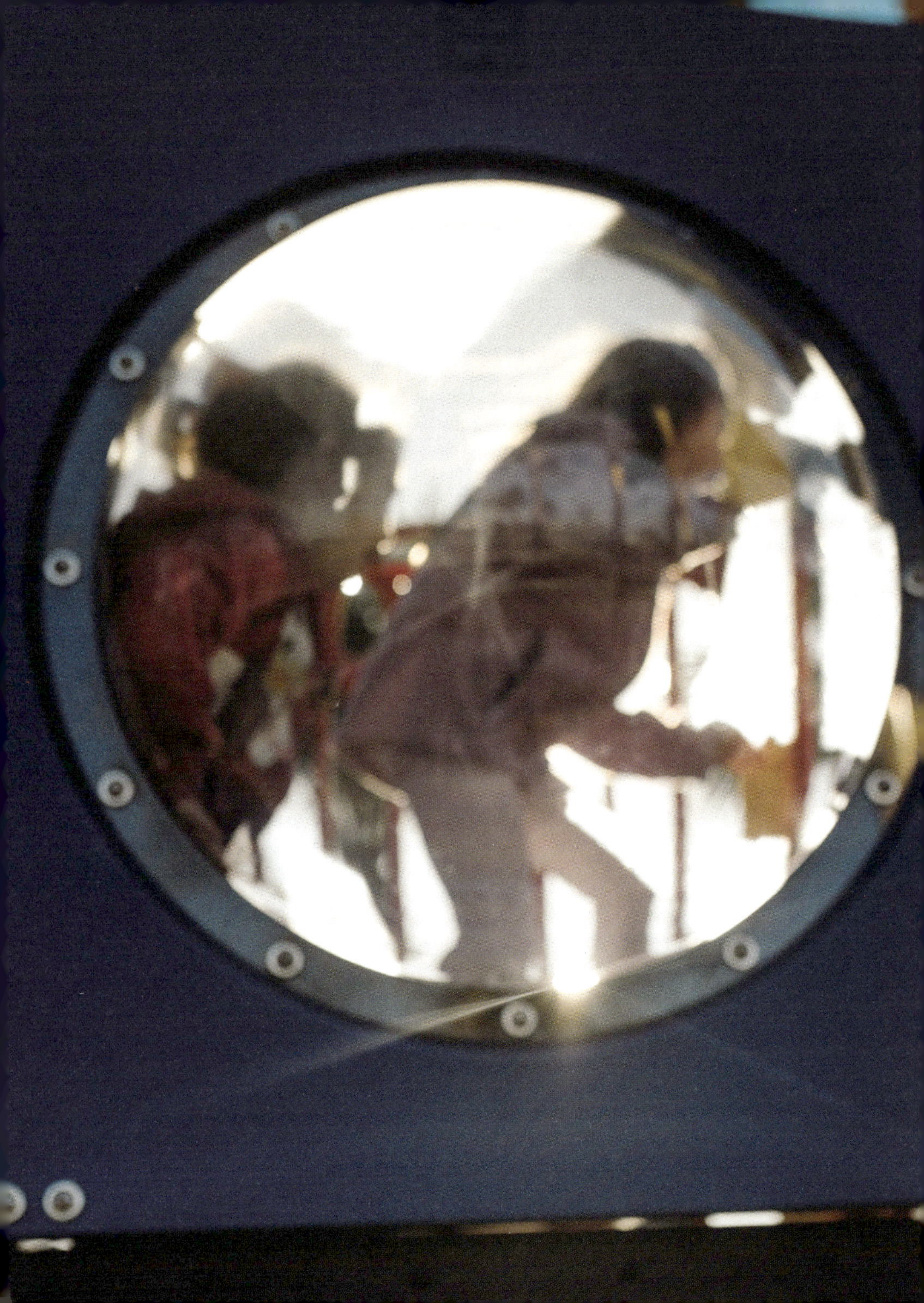

11

What *Can* She Have?

BECKY MORQUECHO

I'm standing in a buffet line at my daughter's American Heritage Girls awards banquet. The long expanse of connected church tables is covered with white linen tablecloths and silver warming dishes filled with chicken tenders, barbecue-glazed meatballs, and mounds of macaroni and cheese. Children on tiptoes peek into each dish as though discovering a treasure, deciding which delicacy will fulfill their immediate desires. Crock-Pots and casseroles boasting tongs and ladles call out: *Take what you want!*

For those who can, that is.

For those who can't, my heart sinks.

I intuitively scan the stretch of tables for more fruits and veggies—other than the ones I brought from home—but walk back to the round table where my family is sitting, carrying a mostly bare paper plate. And carrying a mostly bare sense of belonging on my child's behalf.

I unpack my seven-year-old daughter's black outer space lunch cooler and add homemade veggie meatballs, low-protein rice, and jackfruit "bacon" to the sliced strawberries from the buffet. *Will adding different foods to the same kind of plate help ease the sadness I'm feeling?* I wonder.

Just one or two at first, and then flocks of children dart for the dessert table to find fudgy brownies, chocolate chip cookies, and lemon bars. Any kid's dream. Little girls—some with painted fingers, others with dirt under their nails, all of them with wide eyes—contemplating, reaching, and picking their favorite sugary treats. Delighting in desserts. Without knowing it, delighting in the freedom to do so.

As I watch my daughter watching them, it feels like the left and right sides of my heart are separating, pulling away from one another. I've come armed, as if ready for battle, with homemade low-protein cookies and brownies my daughter *can* have. But that is not a remedy—*is there one?*—for what's happening inside of my chest.

The reality is that all my efforts, preparations, and hours spent in the kitchen can't erase my daughter's strict dietary needs or cushion her longing to grab whatever she wants from a buffet—without checking with me first, without it being something *I* made.

My daughter was born with a rare inherited metabolic disorder that causes phenylalanine, one amino acid of protein, to build up in her body. She'll need to follow a rigorous diet that drastically limits protein for the rest of her life. If she doesn't follow the diet, the disorder can damage her brain.

My daughter's condition may be uncommon, but food limitations are not.

I think about the mamas whose kids have relentless autoimmune diseases, diabetes, or digestive disorders. The ones catering to celiac disease or a life-threatening peanut allergy. A friend of mine has a son with a dairy allergy. She carries an EpiPen and has had to use it because of a mix-up at a gelato shop.

The world is dotted with ice cream shops, cafés, and taco stands. Families are meeting for brunch to celebrate birthdays and graduations. Friends are spontaneously stopping to grab burgers and fries. Sometimes I feel like I'm looking through glass at a make-believe population participating in unattainable traditions and quick, everyday decisions. I feel like I could press my palms or cheek on the window to get close enough to taste that freedom, close enough to fit in, close enough to see my daughter skipping down those seemingly imaginary streets next to the other little girls with vanilla soft-serve cones in hand.

Every now and then, a friend catches a glimpse of my longing through the thick separation between our worlds and moves toward me.

But every now and then, a friend catches a glimpse of my longing through the thick separation between our worlds and moves toward me.

I sit in the sunshine, soaking in the quiet and the scent of orange blossoms, watching my daughter play in a makeshift mud kitchen with my friend Chelsea's daughters. As the dappled light pours through a canopy of branches, my friend walks toward us holding three little bowls of blueberries, one for each mud kitchen chef.

"She has forty-five grams of blueberries," Chels tells me nonchalantly, handing one of the plastic bowls to my daughter.

I exhale relief.

Ten, twenty times a day, I'm weighing snacks. Calculating. Making choices and allowances for what my daughter can eat until a new day

What a relief when someone swoops in and takes over what needs to be done, without me even asking.

begins. Mental math gymnastics, day in and day out, is now involuntary to me, like breath entering and leaving my body.

But what a relief when someone does it for me. What a relief when someone swoops in and takes over what needs to be done, without me even asking.

We're traveling with our friends Shane and Lauren and their kids, caravanning our campers across California. After a long morning of driving, we pull up to Lassen Volcanic National Park. It's June, and the bugs and midday heat are ruthless as we get situated at our home for the night. Our three girls slump onto the worn benches of the picnic table. It's clear that we all need a boost in morale.

Lauren has told me on countless occasions in fewer words: "Yes, my kids can have what your kid is having." She partners with my silent agenda for sameness and solidarity.

I remember the fruit sitting on the Formica counter, next to the panel of retro sunshine wallpaper inside our 1990s RV, and hurry up the steps inside. Anticipation courses through my veins. Such a simple solution. But such a big opportunity.

Minutes later, I walk out of our cozy home on wheels onto the soft forest floor, padded with pine needles. I'm carrying a stained cutting board, every inch of it covered with sliced watermelon.

All three girls cheer.

It's just watermelon, but seeing my daughter's excitement mirrored in her friends' faces, all of them helping themselves without hesitation, gleefully slurping perfect triangles and then reaching for more, is a win. The girls devour the entire wooden slab that was packed to the edges with the juicy pink flesh of watermelon only moments ago.

The kids sit content and satisfied on the sap-covered bench playing cards, with summer's sweetest juice dripping off their chins. A symphony of childhood memories: camping, third-day braids, bug bites, tan lines, dirt-streaked knees, a deck of cards, and a shared snack. At this moment, I know my daughter feels like one of the girls. Not one of the girls with a "special diet."

Simply but profoundly, just one of the girls.

My daughter can't eat a snack-bag of Fritos and more than one Trader Joe's gluten-free chocolate chip cookie on the same day. She definitely can't have chicken, or beans, or tofu, or peanut butter, or store-bought gluten-free bread. She can't have too much broccoli at one time. She can't have more than one hundred grams of tater tots without altering her protein intake for the rest of the day.

"Oh, that's so hard," strangers and new friends say.

Yes, it can be. But also, my daughter's diet doesn't define her. Neither does her observant personality or silly, giggling squeals. Nor does her impressive running endurance, or her gorgeous dark, silky hair. She is a purposefully curated and perfectly created child of God. This specific family limitation can feel all-consuming at times. But I need to be careful not to let it overshadow the brilliant pieces of who we are—of who she is—growing, learning, exploring, and thriving, regardless of what she can't eat.

It's my job to find out what day the third-graders are having yet another party with powdered sugar donuts. It's my job to feed my daughter healthy, life-giving food for her unique body and brain. But when another woman steps into that role in the same manner I would, I feel the left and right sides of my torn and tested heart magnetically move back toward one another to become whole.

Three families are coming to our house for dinner. I both love and hate this. I love foraging for and clipping wild, native plants for centerpieces. I love hearing our kids' laughter bounce and echo off the nearby boulders on our land. I love that we made a downhill Slip 'N Slide that entices toddlers and teens alike, and that we made it out of pond liner and garden irrigation hoses.

But I hate that hosting these families for a meal inevitably means cooking something that my friends, their kids, and my husband and I can scoop into our bowls, but my daughter can't. I hate that she needs to eat a different variation of what the rest of us will have.

Beforehand, my girlfriends ask what they can bring. I ask that whatever they choose, please let me know so I can make something similar for my daughter. They write back, without missing a beat. Callie is bringing a salad. Ivette is bringing a fruit bowl. They already know the diet we must follow.

My heart swells with appreciation.

Then Lindsey texts me separately: *I'm thinking about making this! Does V like carrots?*

It's a recipe specific to my daughter's metabolic disorder. It's a side dish of carrots, sweet potatoes, and sliced apples sweetened with pineapple and brown sugar, salted with coconut aminos, and sprinkled with raisins.

I stand at the kitchen counter and nearly cry.

In the end, my daughter has no idea that Lindsey made a point to include her. In the end, she barely eats any of the carrots. But it isn't really about the carrots.

I guess there *is* an antidote for all the fear, hurt, and pain a mom carries in her heart on behalf of her child with food restrictions.

> **She can have a sense of belonging because her world is full of mothers who notice.**

It's the forty-five grams of blueberries.

It's the commitment to helping other people's children feel included.

It's the text about the recipe.

"So what *can* she have?" strangers and new friends naturally ask next.

She can have your empathy. She can have a seat at the table, adorned with colorful fruit salads and crunchy veggie platters galore. Yes, she can have a hard time with all this. But she can also have French fries. She can have tomatoes, snap peas, and cucumbers from the garden. She can have a few handfuls of popcorn. She can have hope for a future filled with picnics, parties, and celebrations because she longs to live on the inside of the glass.

She can have a sense of belonging—regardless of what's on her plate—because her world is full of mothers who notice.

Watermelon Salad with Mint and Vegan Feta

I have to address the elephant in the room: Does vegan feta taste good? *The answer is yes. It's actually creamier than its dairy-based counterpart. Feel free to swap it with the real thing if you'd like. Either way, making this salad—a quick and colorful addition to any barbecue, pool party, or weeknight dinner—is the way to go instead of letting that watermelon you bought with good intentions sit in your fridge for a week before you throw it away.*

MAKES 6 SERVINGS

6 cups chilled watermelon, cubed
Half a red onion, chopped
1/2 cup vegan feta cheese, crumbled
1/3 cup fresh mint leaves, chopped
Balsamic glaze for drizzling

1. In a large bowl, combine the watermelon, onion, feta cheese, and mint.
2. When you're ready to serve, add the balsamic glaze. Serve chilled!

12

A Long Table

ADRIENNE GARRISON

The fabric was a simple cotton, meant for an A-line skirt or a quilt perhaps. It was forest green with small five-petaled flowers spread across it like buds blown onto the spring grass. I walked along the aisle, my face warm from the breath trapped inside my mask, and touched each pattern, knowing I would eventually find one that drew me in.

For $4.79, I could rip one yard of this fabric four times to create a table runner that, once bonded together with fabric adhesive, would be about thirteen inches wide and twelve feet long. Enough for five women to sit comfortably on either side, with one seat at both ends. Twelve seats to match the vision inside my head—a long table set with glasses reflecting a golden light, dishes and silverware all in a row, chairs empty and waiting. I rang the bell at the cutting counter and listened to it reverberate across paper crafts, home decor, silk florals, and the clearance Easter items. It was early May 2021, and it had been fifteen months since I'd last felt the thrill of my front door opening again and again, receiving the gift of gathering at my table with friends and family.

All humans are born creative, and our outlets are as unique and diverse as we are. It wasn't until the particular art of creating experiences for others had been taken away from me that I realized how essential it was to my self-expression and identity. From *Great Gatsby*–themed book clubs to nineties-themed birthday parties, the joy of anticipating, planning, and bringing a gathering to life had been a mainstay in my adult life across cities and friend groups. In my imagination, this long table sat empty and waiting for so long that part of me began to feel empty as well. As we rounded the corner of one year into a global pandemic, my longing for connection fluttered within me like a moth trapped in a glass jar. I had stopped looking into people's eyes. I no longer knew myself or this world in which we had all become strangers, our homes both fortress and prison, our efforts at connection beautifully inventive yet desperately lacking.

That spring, I allowed the image of the long table to linger longer in my mind. I allowed the ache of loneliness to surface, shaping and funneling it into dreams of an evening of storytelling with women I deeply admired.

YOU ARE INVITED TO A FAITHFULNESS FEAST
Friday, May 7, 2021
6 TO 9 P.M.

Dear friends,

It's been a long year . . .

And yet God has never left our sides. When was the last time you celebrated the faithfulness of God among friends? This will be an evening of heart connection, delicious food, and stories of God's faithfulness in our lives.

Please bring a story of God's provision, presence, or peace in your life this year (off-the-cuff or written down, short or long) and a dish to share.

Let's celebrate His faithfulness together.

Text me with any questions.

Love,
Adrienne

Along with the delicate floral fabric, I requested four yards of medium-weight canvas in an earthy ivory hue to serve as a tablecloth. Six hours before the guests arrived, I left my five- and three-year-old with the remote and Disney+ and began ironing my ad hoc table runner. At five hours till, I filled a zip-top bag with balsamic marinade and several dozen chicken thighs. My husband took over caring for the kids as I set months of dreaming into motion. With the table set and two hours to go, I texted out my address one more time. At thirty minutes till, I put everything into the oven and entered my closet, refusing to let this last and least-joyous decision of what to wear become the evening's crisis. I slipped a silky, long-sleeved shirtdress over my head and stepped past the full-length mirror, barely seeing myself. The menu and outfit seemed beside the point because, for so many months, I'd been waiting simply for this chance to be together.

That evening, with the table stretched the length of my dining room and out into the living room, I lit votive candles and thanked God for this vision made real. I thanked Him for not allowing me to forget—though forgetting would have been so much less painful—the beauty and joy and abundance of sharing a meal.

As my door opened wide to eleven women I adored, the essentials of linens and recipes faded into memory. We dined on stories and laughter, on caramelized green beans, simple brown rice pilaf, and roast chicken. Beth brought a layered peanut butter cake drizzled with caramel and the miraculous details of her son's adoption. April brought a bottle of pinot grigio and the trial of a tense family relationship reconciled after so many years. Sarah brought a charcuterie board and sliced each of us open with the honesty of lingering postpartum depression and the perils of navigating the healthcare system as a Black woman. Tiana, well, she came with two gallons of coveted Chick-fil-A lemonade and somehow, even in the hardship of her own story, brought laughter to the table that left the muscles in my belly aching. I was startled by the deep and ephemeral pleasure of

This gathering was the good and holy work I had been longing for, and my heart felt both lighter and fuller from the gift of it.

being right there, right then, my mind no longer casting out in anticipation for what might be, or longing for what was. Around that long table, we celebrated the gift of God's faithfulness in the present—not at the end of the trials but in the midst of them.

Late into the evening, as my friends began searching for shoes and empty serving dishes, I turned back to the table and saw the beautiful closure of my vision's last brushstrokes completed: chairs askew, candles burned down, folksy floral runner littered with crumbs and crumpled napkins. This gathering was the good and holy work I had been longing for, and my heart felt both lighter and fuller from the gift of it.

At nine o'clock, my guests left in groups of two and three, each of them carrying a tiny golden lantern I had given them as a reminder of the light they bring into my life and the lives of others. I followed the last guests down the sidewalk and stood barefoot in the fading twilight, waving as they drove back to their families. By 10:15, the dishwasher was loaded, the wine glasses gathered by the sink, the floor swept clean. I tossed the napkins in a pile by the washing machine and carefully folded the table runner before climbing, exhausted, into bed.

Within a few months, my handmade table runner had been commandeered by my daughter as a forest floor for fairy dance parties. But when I bumped into April at the pool or Tiana at church, I felt the connection of that evening flicker and glow in the background of our rushed, kid-interrupted conversations. Even now, whenever I see those women, I remember the months of waiting and dreaming, the long table they filled with laughter and story, and the gift of gathering that I no longer take for granted.

No-Sew Table Runner

In my mind's eye, I saw a long, narrow, perfectly set table. In reality, I had two oval-shaped tables to push together for this event. Even with my best attempts, there was a telltale sag in the tablecloth where the rounded edges of the two tables met. But maybe quirks like these—moments when we make the best out of what we have—allow our intentions to be deeply felt all the more by our guests.

MAKES ONE 70-INCH RUNNER, WHICH BEST FITS A 60-INCH TABLE

- 1 yard fabric
- scissors
- iron and ironing board
- ruler
- 10 yards double-sided fusible fabric tape, 1/2-inch wide
- 24 inches scrap ribbon, 1/2-inch wide, optional

1. Fold the fabric in half lengthwise, then cut to make two long pieces.
2. Lay the two pieces of fabric together so that the print-sides of the fabric touch and the back of the fabric is facing out on both sides.
3. On the short side of each piece of fabric, fold over a bit more than 1/2 inch of fabric. Iron this fold to get a sharp crease. Cut your fusible tape to size and place it between the two 1/2-inch folds, pattern side down with the fusible tape between. Iron to create a seam. Now the two halves of your fabric should be joined in the middle.
4. Fold over a bit more than 1/2 inch at each end of the runner and iron to get a sharp crease. Cut your fusible tape to size and place it within the 1/2 seam fold you created. Iron to create a seam. Now each end of your runner should have a finished edge.

5. Repeat the process along the length of each side of the runner by folding over a bit more than 1/2 inch of fabric along each side and ironing it to a sharp crease. Cut fusible tape to size, place within the fold, and iron to seal the seam.

Notes:

When choosing fabric: Cotton or linen is preferred, and medium weight will hold up best.

For easier measuring: If you have some 1/2-inch ribbon on hand, cut 1 to 2 feet of it to use as a measurement tool. The ribbon can help keep your 1/2-inch folds straight, especially for the long side of your fabric. Simply fold the edge of your fabric over the ribbon until it is covered. Ta-da! Keep the ribbon inside while you iron for a sharp crease, then remove it before inserting the fusible tape and ironing a second time.

To create a custom width: The width of your table runner will depend on the width of the fabric you purchase, which may be anywhere from 44 to 60 inches. These directions work best for 44- to 45-inch-width fabric and will produce a runner that is about 21 inches wide. If you'd like a narrower runner, or if your fabric is thicker, simply cut the fabric lengthwise until it is a bit more than 1 inch wider than your preferred width (to account for hems on both sides).

To create a custom length: To adjust this for a shorter or longer table, take the length of your table and add 12 to 18 inches so that the fabric can drape over each side. Divide this number by 2 (since you'll be cutting the fabric in half lengthwise), and request that your choice of fabric be cut to that length.

13

Unexpected Fruit

RUTH GYLLENHAMMER

On a clear, warm December day, we visit the avocado farm for the first time as a family of six. The cottage sits atop a winding driveway like a lookout point beyond which we can see a blue sliver of the glimmering Pacific Ocean. Surrounding us are nearly twenty-three acres of avocado and citrus trees.

My husband and I have always dreamed of owning a property apart from our main home where we could build a family retreat. So when we unexpectedly came across an opportunity to buy land with the potential to be so much more, we jumped at the chance. We call the farm Hope Ranch.

Our newborn daughter—our grand finale girl after three boys—is just five days old when we get the keys. As we walk the property, our boys run free and wild through orange trees and up and down hills. Our daughter, asleep in the crook of my arm, feels tiny and tender. The land is wide and open, and we see only the possibilities.

Looking out onto the valley, an American flag waving in the breeze above me, I recall one of my dad's sayings: "If you're going to dream, you might as well dream in color."

So I do.

Here, by the flagpole and California palms, I envision a large fire pit surrounded by stone seating to roast marshmallows as the sun sets. There, on the empty gravel lot, I picture a row of tiny guest houses and a pickleball court for family weekends. Below, I imagine a renovated pool with a low, built-in waterslide. Next to the house, I see raised cedar garden beds and an outdoor kitchen. Across the driveway, I nurture an image of an artist studio encircled by zinnias.

My vision of hosting extended family weekends, creative retreats, even an annual pool and paella party, feels miraculously within reach. I picture us hosting shrimp boils and Super Bowl parties, with heaping bowls of fresh guacamole and Ina Garten's pink grapefruit margaritas. We are all imagination and optimism and, well, *hope.*

It isn't until we're back in our suburban Orange County home that reality hits. When I open the envelope containing our first water bill, I see the number on the deceptively cheery pink slip of paper, and my stomach drops.

The expenses don't end there. We replace broken irrigation lines. We purchase the nitrogen fertilizer required for organic certification. A windstorm cuts the avocado crop by two-thirds, and it becomes painfully clear that any revenue we'll receive from the avocados will be similarly cut. We discern just how steep the learning curve is for farming.

My mental vision board collides sharply with the numbers I see on the spreadsheets.

Just as quickly as I've blown up the dream in my mind, the bubble bursts, and what I'm left with is what we actually have: the land, the trees, and the fruit.

When the avocados come ready to harvest in February, we have two options: Sell to the packinghouses that process the fruit for grocery stores or take our fruit directly to our community farmer's market.

"Do we really have the bandwidth to spend every weekend at the farmer's market?" I ask my husband.

"It would be a great learning experience for the kids," he replies. "And we might make more money by cutting out the middleman."

We weigh the trade-offs of time and money. We count the cost of commitment. But the decision finally comes down to this: *When else will we have this opportunity as a family?*

And so my husband builds a kid-sized fruit stand out of two-by-fours. I design and print a banner, order an E-Z Up canopy tent, prep a cash box, and open a Venmo account. We task our kids with placing sticker labels on glass juice bottles. We arrange for the fruit to be transported from our farm to our home.

On a still-dark Sunday morning in April, I help my husband load our old Land Rover, recently repainted an avocado-inspired green, with dozens of crates of oranges, lemons, grapefruit, and avocados. He leaves first to set up the tables, canopy tent, and crates. I meet him there with our four kids in tow, including our five-month-old daughter strapped to my chest.

To my great surprise, I love working the farmer's market. I love the bustle of the market and seeing the friendly and familiar faces of our neighbors. I love how our friends come straight from church to support us. I love trading with the other vendors at market close, where we exchange our avocados for ripe strawberries, freshly baked sourdough, and baskets of vegetables. I'm high on the feeling that we're offering something valuable to our community, and we're doing it as a family.

Our eldest boys, ages seven and nine, enthusiastically take turns counting out change and arguing over who gets to wear the Venmo lanyard. My

I'm high on the feeling that we're offering something valuable to our community, and we're doing it as a family.

youngest boy, Micah, with his messy light brown hair and Boston Red Sox jersey, stands in the middle of the market, a giant lemon in one hand and a bag of avocados in the other. He's tiny and tan, beaming as he thrusts avocados toward anyone who smiles in his direction. And who can say no? He's our biggest salesperson—besides our daughter.

Passersby coo over our baby girl with her oversized green bow headband. They stop by our booth just to see her and end up leaving with avocados and glass bottles of orange juice. We spend all morning smiling and talking and connecting.

We used to walk to the farmer's market. We'd grab breakfast burritos and coffee and sit at the adjacent playground. But *working* the farmer's market? Working the farmer's market takes sacrifice, energy, and *heart.* We are no longer spectators.

When the market ends, we still have crates of avocados left. After we make the three-minute drive back to our cul-de-sac, my boys load up our Red Flyer wagon and walk up and down our street, handing out avocados to neighbors like Oprah giving out cars: "*You* get a bag! *You* get a bag! *You* get a bag!"

We send the boys to school with bags of fruit for their teachers and receive the sweetest thank-you notes in return. Micah's preschool teacher tells us, "I've never had more buttery avocados." We are as delighted by the connections made from sharing our avocados as we are from selling them.

From spring through summer, even though our family rhythm revolves around our farm-grown fruit, I begin to realize there are even greater things growing.

Before we knew we'd buy an avocado farm, the word I had chosen for the year was *fruitful.* By *fruitful,* I really meant *productive.* I was hopeful that the time and energy I was investing into managing my home and my work would pay off. I did not mean literal fruit. I did not mean actual avocados. I had no idea the ways God would use fruit to quietly shape our hearts and shift our perspectives.

The avocado farm brought us closer to our community, but not in the ways I expected. I wanted to invite people into an idyllic farm retreat, a beautifully designed place, a perfectly curated experience. Instead, what I invited people into was a front-row seat to our family circus: the farmer's market mornings where we wrangled rowdy boys while attending to customer-neighbors while shushing a sleeping baby and trying to count out the right amount of change. Instead of bringing friends from the suburbs to the farm, we brought the farm to the suburbs.

Our farmer's market weekends taught our boys how to hustle and do quick mental math, certainly. But more than that, what we learned as a family was that what we already have is more than enough to share.

We came to the farm with high hopes and big dreams for grand hospitality, but what we've experienced since that December day is a more down-to-earth vision of community—one that is humble and grounded. A vision that hinges not on what we could build in the future, but on what we can be faithful to in the present. We thought we were just growing fruit, but all the while, an entirely different kind of growth was happening in our hearts, in our family, and in our relationships. And of all the things we've taken away from the farm, that has been the most unexpected fruit.

Hope Ranch Guacamole

Since owning an avocado farm, I've become—perhaps unsurprisingly—very particular about my guacamole. While you might be tempted to pick up a packet of dried guacamole seasoning mix, fresh ingredients make the creamy avocado taste like the best version of itself. The white onion is both sweeter and milder than other onions, making this recipe friendly for kids sensitive to spiciness.

MAKES 4 SERVINGS

3 medium (or 2 large) Hass avocados
Juice of one lime
One garlic clove, grated
1/3 cup fresh cilantro, chopped
1/3 cup white onion (about 1/4 of a medium onion), diced
2 tablespoons diced jalapeño, seeds removed and finely diced
1 teaspoon kosher salt

1. Pit the avocadoes and scoop out the flesh from the skin.
2. In a medium bowl, mash the avocados and lime juice with a fork.
3. Mix in the garlic, cilantro, white onion, jalapeño, and salt.
4. Adjust ingredients to taste, and serve with your favorite chips.

Notes: Hass avocados are what you'll likely find at grocery stores. Their skins turn black when ripe.

Instead of table salt, I use Diamond Crystal kosher salt, which has larger flakes than table salt. Reduce to 1/2 teaspoon if using table salt.

14

Some Things Can't Be Rushed

KATIE BLACKBURN

STEP 1: *The first step* to a good loaf of sourdough bread—and this is coming from someone who is *not* an expert in the subject—is the starter. A simple one-to-one mix of water and flour, the starter is where all the wild yeast and good-for-your-belly bacteria grow, and it is essential to making your bread rise. You can, of course, make your own starter by putting flour and water into a Mason jar and stirring the mixture together until it is a pasty consistency, and do this again every day for maybe a week until it has developed enough wild yeast to make your bread rise. That process depends on a few things, like the temperature of your kitchen or the weather outside. But with tender and consistent attention, you can bring your own starter to life.

However, I recommend an easier strategy: Get a starter from a trusted friend, someone who has been baking bread for a long time. Let them hand you a jar of starter that has lived a little bit of life already, a starter that is proven, strong, and reliable. Most of the things I am pretty sure of in my life have been handed down from someone I trust.

My friend Annie had been making me sourdough bread for a few years before I finally asked her if she would teach me how to make it myself. As a bread enthusiast, she enthusiastically said yes. We met one morning in her cozy kitchen, where she had all the baking tools and ingredients set out in advance, as if she were Emeril Lagasse ready to teach a studio audience how to make a gourmet loaf of sourdough. She showed me how to feed a starter, how much flour to weigh out, and how she determines if the water is warm enough to make the natural yeast in the flour rise. Once we mixed the first loaf, we set it aside to rise and pulled out another bowl of dough from the fridge that she had made the day before, so we wouldn't miss any steps in the lesson.

She set the dough onto a floured corner of the counter, showed me how she shapes her bread, and made sure I knew how to get the best browned edges: You have to take the lid off your baking vessel for the last part of the cooking time. I listened intently, mentally cataloging every instruction, almost giddy to have this knowledge. But Annie stressed that making sourdough would become my own process, that no two people make bread exactly the same, but each loaf can still turn out great every time. While the bread baked and the irresistible smell of sourdough filled the kitchen, she reminded me of a few key things: Keep the starter near the oven if I could, store the sourdough discard—aka, the excess starter left over after a feeding—in a big Tupperware container in the refrigerator for the endless amount of recipe options I could add it to, and always have parchment paper on hand for easy baking and cleanup.

When I left Annie's house, I had all the baking instructions I needed, a jar of my own starter, a warm loaf of sourdough, and the joy that comes from bonding with a friend over a shared love of carbohydrates.

And more than that, thanks to my friend, I left with the confidence and belief that I, too, could make my own bread.

STEP 2: Once you have a strong sourdough starter, the rest of the bread-making process is pretty simple. Weigh all of your ingredients—starter, flour, water, and salt—on a kitchen scale, and mix them with a wooden spoon, or in a mixer with a bread hook attachment, if you prefer. I find both work just fine, but I like feeling the strength it takes my arm to mix the ingredients myself. The dough will be sticky, but should still pull away from the edges of the bowl—that's usually how I know all my proportions are correct. Place a kitchen towel over your bowl, and then find a nice warm spot for the dough to rest for the next hour. If it's not raining or cloudy outside, I usually put mine on the east-facing windowsill in the kitchen, because the morning sun heats that spot just perfectly. In the winter, I keep the dough near the stove. Sourdough doesn't ask for much, but it does demand the right temperature to work its magic. I feel this is a reasonable request.

For the first few months of my sourdough obsession, I made bread four to five times a week. Each loaf made me feel prouder than the one before. I couldn't stop. I brought sourdough to baby showers and girls' nights, and it's only right to tell you that I mostly ate it myself, right out of the oven with a healthy spread of butter that melted directly into the tiny little holes of the bread. There was something comforting about the predictability of making a loaf of bread, and it served as an emotional foil to the chaos of my life: six kids, one child's severe disability, a recent adoption, and a marriage hanging on by a thread.

One summer morning, I got up early to bake a loaf I had prepared the night before, just so I could pack it in a carry-on bag and bring it on a flight from Washington to California for a picnic on the beach with my best friend. We certainly could have bought a loaf of bread at any grocery store, but I wanted to make it myself, to share something I loved doing with one of my people. Ashlee picked me up from the airport, and we drove straight to the ocean in Carmel, a cozy little beach town nestled into the central California coast. She pulled out white cheddar cheese, salami, strawberries, and peach Moscato from her cooler. I unwrapped a loaf of sourdough from the white kitchen towel it had traveled in.

For two hours, we watched the waves and shared our hearts. Mostly, she listened to me trying to navigate the fragility and uncertainty of a marriage I wanted so badly to survive. There are no real answers for conversations like that, only the ears of someone who cares about what you're saying. Pain wants to be solved, certainly. But I think more than that, pain just wants to be heard. It needs to have a safe place to sit for a while.

So Ashlee and I cried and ate bread and whispered prayers over the cadence of the ocean.

STEP 3: After you've let your dough rest in a warm place for an hour or so, bring it back to your kitchen counter for the stretch and folds. This is the part of the process that can feel complicated, and it often loses people when they are reading the recipe in a book. But stretch and folds are really so simple. Here's what you do: Get your fingertips a bit damp, pull one corner of the bread dough away from the side of the bowl, and stretch it a few inches into the air, then pull it back over the rest of the loaf, almost like pulling a soft blanket up over your toddler to tuck her in to bed at night. Turn the bowl a quarter to the left, grab

another corner of the bread dough, and stretch and fold again. Then another turn, and another stretch and fold. One more time, four total. The whole process takes no more than sixty seconds. You're smoothing out the dough with each turn, which you will quickly see as you stretch. But you're also helping the gluten develop, an essential step to ensure the quality of the bread.

Do this whole series of stretches and folds three more times, one hour apart each time. This four-hour process is called the *bulk fermentation*, and you cannot skip or rush it. The repeated rest, rise, stretch, fold, rest rhythm is critical. Skipping this part will result in something that resembles a hockey puck, not a loaf of bread (ask me how I know). So be patient. Then shape your loaf as desired and let it ferment in a bread proofing basket overnight in the refrigerator.

The process is not complicated, but it cannot be rushed. Tend to the bread when needed, but then let time do what only time can do.

When my marriage ended, I put my sourdough starter in the refrigerator. I didn't have much of an appetite, but I also knew that after making sure my kids had everything they needed each day, there wasn't much left of me. Grief is heavy and demanding. As much as I loved making bread—loved the act of creating—I knew I needed to put the practice away for a while. I needed to free up my hands in order to carry all the other pieces of my life around.

A sourdough starter can be kept in the refrigerator, unfed and unused, for months at a time. Some people even say years, but I can't confirm that with experience. What I can say is that when life is really challenging and really painful, the work of healing is all the work we can do. Everything else can wait for a while.

STEP 4: The final step to sourdough is the best part—the baking. I use the same cast-iron pans that I cook with, but if you have a nice Dutch oven, you can use that instead. Put your chosen cooking pan (with its lid) in the oven to preheat at 500 degrees. Once it's nice and hot, carefully take out the pan, place your bread dough on a sheet of parchment paper, then set both into the hot pan. Score (a fancy way of saying "cut") the top of your bread as desired so the steam can escape, which helps the loaf bake correctly. I do one long cut in a crescent moon shape around the side and a few artsy leaf-life scores slightly off-center on the top. You can cut whatever pattern you like. Turn the oven down to 450 degrees, and bake for twenty minutes covered and another twenty minutes uncovered. Like Annie said, that's how you get the crisp edges on the crust.

I'm probably supposed to say that next you should take the loaf out of the oven and let it rest at least thirty minutes before serving. But by this point, you've spent anywhere from twelve to twenty-four hours on this bread, and waiting is hard. I tend to give it five minutes. Then I cut the end off to slather in butter and treat myself to what might be the most delicious and well-earned bite of food in the world.

Several months after my divorce, I had sold my house, moved with my six children to a home with my parents, and generally had been doing only enough to carry my grief and all the other responsibilities of my life from one day to the next day. But one morning, as I moved a few items around in what was still a new-to-me refrigerator in a new-to-me home, I saw my sourdough starter on the top shelf.

It had been an impossibly hard and disorienting few months—actually, five years, when I really think about it. No one could have told me when I'd feel better, but the people in my life knew that. They let God work in the pain in ways only He can. They checked in after my counseling appointments and processed with me how I was naming and acknowledging the losses in my life. They made food for me and cleaned my house and sent me flowers and stared out over ocean waves with prayers for mercy.

And in all of that tending, they trusted that I would one day feel happy again—that I was not a lost cause of despair. But they seemed to understand, long before I did, that joy would return when it was good and ready, and not a minute before.

Joy would return when it was good and ready, and not a minute before.

That time would do what only time could do.

On the morning I saw that sourdough starter on the shelf, I smiled. I knew right then that it was time to bring it back to life.

I placed the jar on the counter and let it come to room temperature. After an hour or so, I scraped off the top layer of starter dough and threw it away. I put the remaining quarter-cup of starter on my kitchen scale and added fifty grams of good bread flour and fifty grams of water. When you're bringing a sourdough starter back from a few months of hibernation, you're looking to bring it from a thick, pasty consistency to a light, bubbly one. But be patient—this might take you a few tries. By the next day, my starter looked the same as it had when I pulled it out of the refrigerator.

So I took a little more starter out of the jar to make room for more flour and water, then fed it again and waited a few hours. Then I did it again.

It took two full days and at least three feedings to get my sourdough back to full strength, where it would have enough active yeast to make a loaf rise to the beautiful sourdough shape we all love. Merely forty-eight hours after I decided it was time to start making sourdough again, I walked into my kitchen early in the morning and saw a starter that had doubled in size, bubbly and airy and ready to work—a gracious reminder that just because something needs healing, that doesn't mean it won't find its strength again.

I almost skipped into the kitchen with delight, eager to grab my kitchen scale and get to work.

I made my first loaf of bread in months. Then I texted a picture of that beautiful loaf to Annie, because she gets excited about these things with me. And another picture to Ashlee, because she still remembers what it felt like to sit with me and cry anxious tears on a picnic blanket while the ocean tide slid over the sand in front of us. I cut and served the warm bread to my kids, and all of us thought it was the best thing we had ever tasted.

There really is nothing complex about sourdough bread. And I am still far from an expert in the craft. But I do know this: Sourdough takes time, and patience, and trust in a process you cannot always see. You cannot force sourdough to be ready when it is not strong enough.

But with some care and tending and waiting, it will be.

And so will you.

Sometimes the most important ingredient is simply time.

The Best Italian Dipping Oil

There are truly a hundred ways to enjoy your warm sourdough bread. Ripping off a chunk before anyone else cuts into it and slathering that piece in butter before I even sit down might be my favorite. But sometimes I practice a bit more civility. Sometimes I actually let the loaf cool down as long as it is supposed to, slice it carefully with a serrated knife, set the bread in a basket, and serve it with this flavorful dipping oil. Even if there are still dishes in the sink and crumbs on the floor, you'll feel for a brief moment like your kitchen table turned into a fancy restaurant. And I think from time to time, that's a little gift we can give ourselves.

MAKES 1 1/4 CUPS

1 tablespoon black pepper
1 tablespoon dried thyme
1 tablespoon dried mint
1 tablespoon dried oregano
1 tablespoon garlic powder
3 garlic cloves, minced
1 teaspoon sea salt
1 teaspoon red pepper flakes
1 cup extra-virgin olive oil
1/4 cup balsamic vinegar

1. In a small bowl, combine the black pepper, thyme, mint, oregano, garlic powder, garlic cloves, salt, red pepper flakes, and olive oil. Let the mixture sit at room temperature until ready to serve.
2. Just before serving, drizzle balsamic vinegar into the oil.
3. Dip warm, crusty bread in the oil and enjoy every bite.

Note: This recipe is adapted from the *Complete Charcuterie* cookbook.[1]

15

The Proof Is in the Show Notes

ASHLEE GADD

"All right, what are we ordering?" someone asks over the sound of shuffling menus and water pouring into five glasses.

It's 6 p.m. on a Thursday night, I am wearing hard pants, and all is right with the world.

As always, our table hosts the same cast of characters. First, there's Dana, a bona fide doctor, and the smartest one in our group by far. She always comes to dinner straight from work, wearing some adorably chic outfit paired with heels (at four foot eleven, we do not fault her for this). Next to Dana sits Anna: perpetually tan, fit, hair like a mermaid. She's our best storyteller, clever and witty, most likely to be hopping on a plane to Portugal next month. Then there's Kat, animated and full of life, whose infectious laugh can be heard clear across a crowded restaurant. She's the chillest mom you've ever met, most likely to hand her kids an axe with no instructions. Kara rounds out the table with the energy of a caffeinated puppy, best known for turning strangers into friends and her severe lack of tech savviness. (Once, after Anna had just started dating someone post-divorce, we looked up his Instagram profile on Kara's phone and she clicked "follow" like it was no big deal. We will never let her live this down.)

And then there's me. In addition to my excellent TV and skin care recommendations, I am most likely to complain about the parking anytime someone suggests we meet downtown. We have a running joke that the title of my future memoir will be *I Was Told There'd Be Parking.*

We pass a plate of bacon-stuffed croquettes around the table and sample each other's drinks, an underrated act of familiarity. While you can certainly forge a friendship anywhere these days, for our little group, being out in the world together is part of our rapport. We're committed to our collective friendship, yes, but we're also committed to patronizing our local restaurants, leaving generous tips, and supporting the chefs and servers and farmers who make up the ecosystem of our beloved city, Sacramento.

The conversation flows effortlessly as we hop from topic to topic: the perils of raising teenagers, work drama, home repairs, caring for aging parents, and everything we're learning in therapy. We cover the highs and lows of our very real lives and then switch gears to the current state of denim, perimenopause, that funny viral TikTok (worth noting: none of us have TikTok), and the question of the day: *Is at-home laser hair removal worth trying?*

We order dessert because Dana always wants dessert. The server sets a molten chocolate lava cake in the middle of the table with five spoons. And then, before the check comes, Anna prompts us to get out our calendars. We all grab our phones and toss out a handful of dates, looking for the unicorn of a night that will work for all of us. After a few rounds of *I'm out of town that week* and *I have book club that night*, we land on April 17. Kara opens her Notes app and consults a list of restaurants we haven't tried yet. As always, I cast my vote for the option with the best parking.

After we plug the details into our calendars, Dana slides her credit card into the folder with the bill. Anna crunches the numbers and tells everyone how much to Venmo. We all slip outside into the dark and give quick hugs, reminding each other what links to put in the "Show Notes"—which is what we call our group text. We split off in different directions toward our cars, feeling lighter even though our bellies are full.

In four weeks, we'll do this all over again and pick up right where we left off.

In our early twenties, this same group of women rotated weekly through each other's living rooms, devouring Christian authors like Beth Moore and Tim Keller, occasionally studying entire books of the Bible. We sprawled out across couches with hot mugs of tea in our hands and plates of cookies on the coffee table, studying gospel buzzwords like *grace* and *mercy* and discussing what those terms actually meant. One quarter, we took a break from curriculum altogether, opting instead to share when and how we each became believers. I cannot possibly overstate how profoundly those conversations impacted my faith and set the foundation for this friend group. That Bible study ran like clockwork for a number of years, organized by three women who eventually all moved away.

Those of us left behind were busy having babies, establishing careers, and trying to keep our heads above water. None of us felt equipped or had the capacity to step into the role of leadership. Unfortunately—without formal administrators selecting the studies, curating discussion questions, and spearheading logistics—the entire thing fell apart. We all got busy. Time passed. Life moved on.

Until one day when Dana texted: *I miss you guys.*

Someone else typed: *Same. Should we grab dinner soon?*

I don't remember where we went or what we ate. All I remember is this: At the end of the meal, Anna prompted us to pull out our calendars and plan the next one. So we did. Five weeks later, we met up again at a different restaurant. By that point, we already knew the drill. Before the check arrived, we set the next date.

Eating dinner together once a month might not sound like much, but when I consider the depth of what we've navigated together—pregnancies, loss, divorce, unemployment, not to mention a global pandemic and three toxic elections in which we did not all vote the same—you can cover a lot of emotional ground in twelve uninterrupted meals a year.

I still remember the night I quietly pushed a piece of chicken around my plate. I had just given birth to my daughter, Presley, and didn't feel like myself. When the word *depressed* finally toppled out of my mouth, weighty and abrupt, everyone put down their forks. I'll never forget that specific sound—*clank, clank, clank*—a chorus of compassion. Likewise, I'll never forget the night Anna told us her marriage was over. We ate tacos in the backyard and listened like we've never listened before. *Are you sure?* we asked. Every single one of us cried when she nodded yes.

Sandwiched in between every big, heavy discussion are a hundred ordinary ones: lighthearted chitchats about upcoming vacations and college reunions and the hilarious things our kids are saying. These dinners form a kaleidoscope of memories: scenes of truffle fries and prosecco, confessions and inside jokes, twinkle lights and cozy leather booths. We share occasional tears, yes, but also an abundance of laughter—"Carbonated holiness," as Anne Lamott says[1]—all set to the same soundtrack: a melody of ambient music, clinking glasses, and the distinct pitch of silverware eagerly scraping across butter-drenched plates.

Within this group, our concentric circles don't overlap much. We live in different neighborhoods, and our kids go to different schools. We don't all attend the same churches or work out at the same gyms. We don't even shop at the same grocery stores. Had we never committed to a monthly dinner, I believe all these women would still be in my life, but likely more as acquaintances or the kinds of friends who, over time, simply drift apart.

I've been on countless text threads where *We should hang out sometime!* is both a regular refrain and an empty promise. I'm learning that this is the difference between friend groups that last for seven years and those that don't: Friend groups that last actually *do*, indeed, hang out sometime.

If friendship is an investment, this group has the receipts. We make small but significant deposits into one another's lives every month. Every time we plug a fresh date into the calendar, every time we squeeze our bodies into hard pants, every time we scramble out of our homes and offices to venture across town and fight for a parking spot (ugh!), we are whispering to one another: *This matters.* You *matter. And* you *matter. All of you matter to me.*

After we had been meeting for a while, our monthly dinners went on to inspire new traditions. Like every February, when Anna hosts us at her house for "Galens-gras"—a mashup of Galentine's Day and Mardi Gras, when we feast on jambalaya and Dana brings king cake, a small tribute to her time living in New Orleans. For our December meal, we always dress up—occasionally sporting sequins and red lipstick—in celebration of Anna's and Kara's birthdays. One December we even tacked on a Taylor Swift–themed candlelight concert. (At first glance Kara didn't read the text correctly and thought we were *actually* seeing Taylor Swift. At the train museum. For thirty dollars a ticket. Again, we will never let her live this down.)

If friendship is an investment, this group has the receipts.

I'm tempted to tell you there's nothing special about us. We are just five women. Five mothers. Five friends. Then again, maybe this *is* special, the fact that we treat our friendship like a real commitment. Our monthly dinner isn't a placeholder on the calendar, something we can easily cancel at the last minute if a better option comes along. If anything, we consider our monthly dinners nonnegotiable—not because we're rigid about it, but because we are genuinely committed to bearing witness to one another's lives.

> **We consider our monthly dinners nonnegotiable—not because we're rigid about it, but because we are genuinely committed to bearing witness to one another's lives.**

We are all in—fully devoted to showing up, to sustaining our inside jokes, to making space for one another around a table on a regular basis. This formula is not sexy, but it's also not complicated: Consistency is the glue holding us together.

It's dinner, but it's more than dinner. It's the kind of collective friendship that deepens and grows over time, over pizza and good company, over burgers and pork chops and epiphanies and tears, over countless nights laughing until your abs hurt. It's dinner, but *it's so much more than dinner.* It's like a Polaroid developing, slowly, gradually. You just have to wait, and wait, and keep showing up every month, over and over, until the picture gets a little clearer, a little more defined, until one day you can finally see all the colors and you realize, *I can hardly remember my life without these women, without these dinners.* The sum is better than the parts. And I mean that in terms of us, our actual selves, and also in the sheer hours we've logged together.

It almost sounds too good to be true that simply plugging a date into your calendar once a month could lead to seven years of steady friendship, but the proof is in the Show Notes. One scan of our group text would display a full archive of where we've eaten and what we've talked about, plus a mix of prayer requests, memes, and countless references to inside jokes nobody but us would understand.

I don't believe in friendship hacks, but I believe in this: Consistency is a superpower.

Set the date. Show up. Before you leave, plan the next one.

Dinner is our thing, but the formula works with any kind of gathering: afternoon playdate at the park, a scenic walk along the river, brewing coffee at home in soft pants. The *how* and *when* and *where* are not nearly as important as the *why*.

As Anna always reminds us, "Together is the point."

Bougie Popcorn

Going out to a restaurant might not always be possible, so here's a recipe for the nights when you and your friends opt to stay in: popcorn, but make it bougie. Who knew truffle oil and nutritional yeast could be such a dream team? This snack pairs well with a giant couch, your favorite sweatpants, honest conversations, and Georgia's Famous Fudge (page 52).

MAKES 12 TO 14 CUPS

1 tablespoon olive oil
1/2 cup popcorn kernels
2 tablespoons butter
1 tablespoon truffle oil
3 tablespoons nutritional yeast
1 teaspoon garlic powder
1/2 teaspoon sea salt, plus more to taste

1. Place a large, heavy-bottomed pot on the stove. Add the olive oil and 3 popcorn kernels to the pot, and place a lid on top. Turn the heat to medium-high. When you hear the kernels pop, add the 1/2 cup popcorn kernels, turn the heat down to medium, and put the lid back on. I like to keep the lid propped open ever so slightly to let steam out. Be careful not to open it too much, as piping hot kernels might shoot across your kitchen (ask me how I know).
2. Once the popping starts, carefully grasp the sides of the pot with potholders and give it a gentle shake every minute or so (this helps prevent burning). When the pops start to slow down (about 8- to 10-second lapses in between), remove the pot from the heat.
3. Add the butter and truffle oil. Put the lid back on and shake the pot.

4. Open the lid and sprinkle the nutritional yeast, garlic powder, and sea salt over the popcorn. Put the lid back on and shake the pot again. Taste the popcorn and see if it needs more truffle oil or salt. Add accordingly, and serve immediately.

Note: This recipe is fully customizable and impossible to mess up (unless you burn it). Not a fan of nutritional yeast? Swap that for true cheddar cheese powder. Need this to be dairy-free? Swap the butter for more olive oil or a butter substitute.

16

Branding Season

CARA STOLEN

It isn't just the Nikon slung around his neck that sets him apart. No, what I initially notice about him as he strides across the pasture toward the branding pen is his shoes: clean low-tops that are completely unsuitable for a cow pasture. I knew that a photographer for the Washington State Beef Commission was coming to our branding, but when he reaches out to shake my husband's hand, I feel like I'm watching a scene from a movie where a present-day city-dweller is transported to the Old West. His T-shirt and dark-wash jeans are a stark contrast to the boots, chaps, pearl-snap shirts, and cowboy hats everyone else is wearing. We've already started the branding process when he arrives. The crew is working through the calves quickly, and I figure we'll be done with our small, eighty-head herd of cattle by early afternoon. When it's my turn to shake the photographer's hand, he makes a comment about my hands being full. At first, I think he must mean my three kids—it's a statement moms of multiples hear a lot—but then I realize he means it more literally. I'm standing with a vaccine gun in each hand and my one-year-old, Reid, in a carrier on my back.

"Do all these people own these cows together?" he asks.

I cock my head and wonder what he means. "No, just my husband, Levi, and me?" I finally answer, half question, half statement.

"Oh," he says. "So what is everyone doing here? Does everybody just come to help?"

I pause, pondering his question, then consider the scene in front of me with an outsider's lens.

Two cowboys on horseback wrangle a calf out of the herd with ropes, and then two more cowboys run out and pull the calf to the ground. A woman with a baby on her back pokes the calf in the neck twice with needles while another woman shoves a tube in the calf's mouth and pours a blue substance down its back. Then a five-year-old girl rubs a pink paint stick on the calf's nose and yells, "He's done, Dad!"

Back out of the line of fire, I hear the photographer's camera shutter click a few times and remember he's still standing next to me. I don't actually know how to answer his question.

I could explain the significance of livestock brands, which are used to denote ownership and are placed in a specific location on the cow or calf's body with a hot iron. I could tell him how brands are registered with the state, regulated by the USDA, and can be traced back to 2700 BC. But a branding is bigger than a branding iron. It's an event—a time-honored tradition in Western culture when a group of calves receive their brand and first round of vaccines.

Historically, brandings required more hands than the number of cowboys on any given ranch, and hired day help was cost prohibitive in an industry with such small profit margins. So the tradition included asking neighboring ranchers to come and help with the branding, accompanied by the offer to return the favor when the time came for their own livestock. And every year for decades, those neighbors did, in fact, show up for one another, sometimes traveling for a whole day on horseback to do so.

Today, many ranchers brand and vaccinate their calves by running them through a chute or using a calf table. But, lacking the financial resources of a big operation, we prefer the old way. Branding day isn't just about getting your calves branded and vaccinated. It's a celebration of cows getting turned out on grass for the summer and getting back all the time and money you spent feeding them hay through the winter. It's a chance to gather with your friends and neighbors after a long, dark season. It's an opportunity to participate in a centuries-old tradition and preserve a piece of heritage.

So, every April, when green grass peaks through crackling, dormant stalks and the wind starts to blow—when the snow begins to disappear from the hills and the air carries the first glimmer of spring—the texts and phone calls with branding invitations start to fly.

> **Then he grinned and waved at me, shouting, "Love you, Mom!" over his shoulder as he jumped down the porch steps and ran to the pickup to go gather our cows with Levi.**

I could tell the photographer about legacy, and how branding season is an opportunity for this community to pass on their knowledge and skills to the next generation. I could explain how excited my seven-year-old son, Royce, was when we told him our branding was coming up. I could describe how thrilled he was that we let him skip school today and how he laid out his favorite button-up "cowboy shirt" and best jeans for the occasion last week. He'd been dressed and ready when I stuck my head in his room at six o'clock this morning and happily loaded the roast beef sandwiches I made into a cooler while I put the finishing touches on a coffee cake.

Then he grinned and waved at me, shouting, "Love you, Mom!" over his shoulder as he jumped down the porch steps and ran to the pickup to gather our cows with Levi.

In the pen, our friend Jorge pulls a small calf out of the herd. "You ready, Royce?" he hollers.

My heart stops a little. I've known this day was coming—when Royce would rope calves with the big boys, but, as with so many things in parenting, now that the moment's here, I'm not ready.

Royce has been riding his horse independently since he was four and swinging a rope at the roping dummy since before he could talk. He's been practicing his roping all spring in preparation for this moment. But when he trots his horse behind the calf and swings his loop overhead, I turn my back to the pen, unable to watch.

When I finally turn to look, the loop of Royce's rope is pulled tight around the calf's feet—the look on his face says it all. And riding on either side of him, their horses close to protect him, I see our friend Ryan and one of our neighbors. Royce isn't their son. They have no obligation to help him. Yet in the branding pen, the kids belong to everyone. We all play a part in imparting this tradition, these skills, to the next generation. The sight has me swallowing tears.

I could explain to the photographer the significance of the moment we just witnessed and how scary it was for me to watch, knowing full well how dangerous roping can be. Or I could tell him how ranching—or any agricultural vocation for that matter—isn't for the faint of heart. I could describe our long hours, our struggle to make ends meet, and how we don't go on summer vacations like our kids' friends. I could explain how, despite knowing our work is important, we often feel overlooked and invisible. But on branding day, it all feels worth it. At a branding, we get to participate in a community that shows up for one another. We get to model for our kids what it looks like to participate in a long-standing tradition where everyone has a role to play (even if mine looks more like time in the kitchen than swinging a rope).

I watch the crew work together in a familiar yet un-orchestrated rhythm and think about how, to an outsider—to the photographer standing next to me—it probably *does* look like this is a team of people who work together every day. As each calf is pulled out of the herd, the group works together in an improvised dance of sorts, anticipating each other's movements and reacting to them in turn.

There are whoops and hollers when a roper makes a particularly impressive catch and collective groans when a rope slips off a calf's foot at the last second. The sun comes out from behind the clouds, and everyone's shirts darken with sweat. Coolers creak as water, soda, and Gatorade are retrieved. Laughter and good-natured teasing mix with the sound of calves bawling. It's a party, with a hefty dose of hard work.

It's the same as every other branding I've ever been to through the years. The same as it will be at Ryan's next Tuesday. The same way it was at the branding last week. The same way it will be throughout branding season this year, and next year, and the year after that. The same way it's been for a hundred years or more.

Looking around the pen, I'm proud to be part of this tradition. I'm grateful to raise my kids in this community where neighbors both give and accept help from one another freely, and cowboys, who might seem a little rough around the edges to an outsider, ride across the pen to protect someone else's little boy.

This group has celebrated birthdays together at brandings. We've shown up at the last minute when someone rescheduled due to rain. Levi has driven across the state to help someone he knew was shorthanded. And a few years ago, when one of our valley's most beloved cowboys was fighting a losing battle with cancer, our community showed up to brand his calves for him while he watched from the sidelines for the first time in his life.

This is a community rooted in a lifestyle—a lifestyle built on helping your neighbor.

The pace of the branding begins to slow as the ropers try to sort the last few calves out of the bunch. I put the lid on the pan of coffee cake—now just crumbs—and place it on the back seat of the pickup, along with the empty coffee carafe. Royce rides into the pen one last time and turns the cows and their calves back out into the pasture. One by one, the crew makes their way over to the vaccine tables, and my friend Katie and I lay out home-grown roast beef sandwiches, store-bought cookies, and a box of single-serving chips.

The kids, whose hands all show signs of marking calves with the pink paint stick, ask to eat their cookies first like they do every year. The cowboys each grab a sandwich, then sink onto closed cooler lids or lean against stock trailers. Our neighbor Steve asks me how irrigating is going and if I have time for one of his pastures. Everyone teases Royce for how filthy he is and compliments him on his "nice catch." Someone offers the photographer a sandwich, and someone else asks him where he's from.

It isn't until the photographer makes the rounds shaking hands and saying goodbyes that a thought occurs to me: I got caught up in the momentum of the day and never told him any of those things I was thinking of. Glancing around at the familiar group of faces, I hope the day spoke for itself.

Branding season is about community, tradition, and the legacy of both. It's about living the old adage that *many hands make light work.* And it's about the simple pasture meal we share together—an inadequate thank-you of sorts—before everyone goes back to their own little corners of the valley.

Simple Roast Beef for Sandwiches

More a method than an actual recipe, this roast beef turns out perfect every time. I implore you to buy your beef from a local rancher or farmer. I know it feels intimidating, but if you visit your local farmer's market and ask around, I can almost guarantee you can find a family selling beef. Not only will the quality be better, but you'll also be supporting a family like mine in the process!

SERVES 4

1 4-pound sirloin tip roast
4 cloves garlic, minced
Black pepper

Note: You can substitute sirloin tip roast with other cuts like top round, bottom round, or eye of round if those are more readily available. Also, a cooling rack set in a foil-lined sheet pan can be used in place of a roasting pan.

1. Preheat the oven to 325 degrees.
2. Remove the roast from its packaging, pat dry, and trim any excess fat. Rub roast all over with garlic and black pepper.
3. Place the roast on a rack in a shallow roasting pan. Do not cover the roast, and do not add water to the pan.
4. Cook the roast until its internal temperature reaches 145 to 155 degrees, depending on desired doneness. Remove the roast from the oven and tent with foil for an additional 10 minutes. If you intend to eat the meat that day, slice and serve.
5. To use the roast for Branding Day Roast Beef Sandwiches (page 147), let the roast cool on the countertop for 30 minutes, then place in the fridge to cool completely. Once cool, wrap tightly in foil and return to the fridge. Slice just prior to making sandwiches. Use within 3 days.

Branding Day Roast Beef Sandwiches

Since the morning of Branding Day is usually hectic, I always make our roast beef sandwiches the night before. To make ahead, simply assemble the sandwiches, set each on a folded paper towel, then wrap them individually in tin foil before putting them all in the fridge. When you're ready to leave, toss the sandwiches in a cooler, and away you go!

MAKES 4 COWBOY-SIZED SANDWICHES

- 4 ciabatta rolls
- 6 tablespoons mayonnaise
- 4 teaspoons creamy horseradish
- 1 pound roast beef, thinly sliced
- 1 cup banana peppers, drained and blotted
- Optional toppings: sliced cheese, iceberg lettuce, Dijon mustard, pepperoncini

1. Using a bread knife, slice the ciabatta rolls horizontally.
2. In a small bowl, combine the mayonnaise and horseradish. Spread the mixture onto both sides of each roll.
3. Add the roast beef to the bottom half of each roll, followed by the banana peppers. Add any other toppings, if using. Top each sandwich with the other half of the ciabatta roll to close.
4. Serve immediately, or set each sandwich on a folded paper towel, then wrap in foil and place in the fridge until ready to eat.

Note: If you'd like to change up the recipe, use Dijon mustard on one half of the sandwich instead of horseradish mayo, add sliced cheddar or lettuce, and use pepperoncini or pickles in place of banana peppers. On Branding Day, I usually make several of these variations so I can offer options to our crew!

THE KINGDOM
COLLECTION

17

Collateral Damage

SARAH J. HAUSER

I'm standing in the guest room at a family friend's house, rifling through my suitcase to find the shirt my toddler needs. My laptop sits open on the bed, and my son is lying on his stomach in front of it, hands propped under his chin, giggling at Bluey and Bingo and the silly antics of cartoon dogs playing on the screen.

A few months ago, my husband and I decided to relocate. Instead of house-hunting with our entire motley crew, which would have required my eldest three children to miss school and my husband to take off work, my two-year-old and I left the rest of them in Illinois and flew to North Carolina in search of a new home. My son and I are staying with longtime family friends who happen to live in the next town over from where we're looking to move. This couple has known me since I was in seventh grade and feel almost like an aunt and uncle. We've stayed connected over the course of decades, and they've kindly offered their place as a home base for us during the moving process.

This will be easy, I had thought a couple days earlier as I packed our bags. *I'll only have one kid with me instead of all four*. But that one kid loves to climb and run and make messes. And so today, standing in the guest room, with my back turned momentarily as I dig through our luggage, that child shimmies off the bed, feet first, to get down. Except he's too far toward the top of the bed and slides down at an angle where his feet meet the lamp sitting on the nightstand. It hits the floor with a crash, the lamp shattering into hundreds of pieces.

The sound of the breaking glass startles me, and I turn around to see the cause.

"Sam! No!"

Oh shoot, oh shoot, oh shoot.

My heart races and my eyes dart back and forth, taking inventory of the amber-colored pieces all over the floor.

Did I mention that this home is beautiful—stunning, actually—and that many of the items in the home are one-of-a-kind antiques, carefully collected and curated over decades?

In other words, *Did my son just break an irreplaceable treasure?*

There is no fixing it, just cleaning to do. I move my son to the other side of the room where he won't get cut by the shards, then find a broom and vacuum in the downstairs closet. My heart continues to race. The tears start to fall. A knot forms in my stomach. As I sweep, I rehearse in my mind what to say when our friends arrive back home. I text my husband about what happened so he can mentally prepare for the replacement lamp we'll need to purchase.

The minute our hosts walk in the door, I meet them in the entryway and burst into tears. "I'm so sorry!" The words gush out of me like a fire hose as I explain what happened. "I know that was probably an antique, and we will buy you a new lamp, and I'm so sorry!"

They look at me kindly, their eyes wide with surprise—not because of the incident but because of my response. They shake their heads with a smile, and one of them speaks up. "Sarah. It's just a *lamp*."

About a decade ago, before we had kids, my husband and I hosted extended family for Thanksgiving dinner. I planned the menu weeks in advance and, like the organized hostess I wanted to be, tracked what everyone was bringing on an Excel spreadsheet. The night before the holiday, my husband and I moved the couch out of our living room so we could put two tables together, end to end, to fit everyone. I covered the tables with a giant tablecloth, set out the platters and serving dishes we'd need the next day (with labels indicating which piece would be used for which dish), and made sure we had room for every person and every item. The dining room, which was far too small to hold a sit-down meal with the whole family, would be used for appetizers and drinks.

In that dining room, we had a black bar cabinet with doors that swung open a full 180 degrees. You could then pull out an extension piece to sit on top of the opened doors to create a long buffet-style table to use for serving. We set out bottles of wine, glasses, and a few hors d'oeuvres across the top so people could pour a drink and enjoy a few bites before the main course. *Perfect*, I thought as I gingerly pushed the base of a wine glass just so, making sure it lined up perfectly with the rest of the row. I let out a deep breath. *We're ready*.

One by one, families arrived, and before long, the noise of kids and clinking dishes and conversation filled the house. I returned to the kitchen, and as I stirred more butter into the mashed potatoes and poked the turkey with a meat thermometer, I heard a crash. I looked over at our dining room—the room with the white carpet—and saw my elementary-aged niece standing next to the cabinet, red wine and broken glass splayed across the floor in front of her. She had tried to close the cabinet doors without realizing they were holding up the table extension—and therefore the drinks sitting on top of it. When she innocently shifted the door, thinking she was merely closing an opened cabinet, everything above it—an open bottle and wine glasses—came crashing down, the formerly white carpet now looking like a burgundy-colored Jackson Pollock painting.

I was deeply annoyed.

We'd only lived in that house a little over a year, and I hoped the carpets would have stayed white a bit longer. And even though the wine glasses weren't expensive, we only had so many. Not to mention, an entire bottle of wine was now gone, and Lord knows you can't run out of wine at a party.

My own kitchen preparations came to a screeching halt as the cleanup process ensued. My brother-in-law moved his daughter out of the way and started picking up the largest pieces of glass. My husband grabbed the vacuum cleaner, and my sister found the OxiClean under my kitchen sink. I grabbed rags from the cabinet to help, gritting my teeth in frustration and not hiding my annoyance all that well.

There goes my carpet, I thought. I didn't say that, thankfully, but graciousness sure wasn't my default response. Still, I managed to (mostly) hold my tongue. My sister apologized about a thousand times, and while the OxiClean soaked into the carpet, we moved on to enjoy our turkey and stuffing—a wine glass, a bottle of red, and my own attitude the only things worse for wear.

There's a scene at the beginning of *The Hobbit* where a group of dwarves overruns the home of the protagonist hobbit, Bilbo Baggins. Bilbo had sort of reluctantly—and mistakenly—invited the wizard, Gandalf, to tea one day. But when Bilbo answered the door, an uninvited dwarf stood there instead.

Bilbo didn't quite know what to do. He let in the dwarf, and the dwarf quite quickly made himself at home. Then there was another, even louder, ring at the door. Another dwarf stepped in, uninvited, but acting like he was meant to be there all along. The second dwarf asked for beer and cake, and then to Bilbo's surprise, more dwarves rang the bell and entered. Then more and more, until thirteen dwarves, along with the wizard, ended up descending on Bilbo's house asking for coffee and red wine and pork pie and salad and cakes and eggs. "By the time [Bilbo] had got all the bottles and dishes and knives and forks and glasses and plates and spoons and things piled up on big trays, he was getting very hot, and red in the face, and annoyed."[1]

In our neighborhood, there's a group of kids who run around from house to house, playing kickball and raiding pantries and eating at whatever home they land at around mealtime. It's what I dreamed of for my kids. But even though I want my home to be filled with that joyful chaos, sometimes when it's *my* pantry and *my* food and *my* floors that get messier, I'm tempted to react more like Bilbo—red in the face and annoyed. I'm happy to show hospitality when I can plan ahead and the house isn't destroyed and I still have food left. I want the kind of hospitality I have control over. But controlled hospitality can be a selfish version of the welcome we're meant to show.

After ten years, four kids, and a rescue dog since that Thanksgiving incident, I've learned a thing or two about spills. I've learned which carpet cleaners are best and that purchasing a carpet shampooer is 100 percent worth it. I've learned that school-age kids can put Tolkien's dwarves to shame in an eating contest, the pile of shoes by the front door is a beautiful sight, and it's important to keep allergy-friendly snacks on hand so no kid feels left out.

I've also learned, as Tim Chester once wrote, that "hospitality will lead to collateral damage."

"Food will be spilled on your carpet," Chester continued. "You'll be left with clearing up. Your pantry may be decimated. But remember that God is welcoming you into his home through the blood of his own Son. The hospitality of God embodied in the table fellowship of Jesus is a celebration and sign of his grace and generosity. And we're to imitate that generosity."[2]

I wish I had read those words before my niece spilled red wine on my dining room carpet. Maybe I would have handled that situation better. I should have looked her in the eyes and said, without hesitation, "It's just a carpet." Because hospitality doesn't always look like relaxing dinner parties or serene coffee dates. More often, it looks like inviting messy, imperfect people into your messy, imperfect life—and loving one another anyway. It means rifling through the refrigerator to feed the needs of those in front of you and then seeing the pile of dirty dishes as a sign of time well spent. It's about providing a place where people can take a breath, where they can pull up a chair and know, no matter what, they are welcome there.

Hospitality doesn't always look like relaxing dinner parties or serene coffee dates.

Understanding the meaning—and the cost—of hospitality frees me to accept and extend grace in a way I'm not naturally inclined to do. No matter how much I try to control, no matter how good of a guest I try to be, no matter how much I plan and prepare as a host, glasses will break and drinks will be spilled and kids will never have their fill of snacks. Collateral damage comes with the gig. I can spend my energy taking a mental inventory of the messes and losses while gritting my teeth in frustration, or I can grab the carpet cleaner and restock the snack drawer, offering the grace and spirit of welcome that's been generously offered to me.

No-Bake Oatmeal Snack Bites, Two Ways

I often have a stash of these bites in my refrigerator or freezer to feed whatever hungry kids come through the door—or to grab when I need a little sustenance on the go. Feel free to mix and match with other ingredients, such as subbing in dried cherries for the cranberries or using cashew butter instead of almond butter. They're an easy make-ahead snack that helps me feel (slightly more) prepared for impromptu hospitality.

EACH RECIPE MAKES ABOUT 24 BITES

Chocolate Chip Peanut Butter Snack Bites

2 cups rolled oats

1 1/2 cups creamy peanut butter

3/4 cup mini chocolate chips

1/4 cup honey

1/4 cup chia seeds

1/4 teaspoon kosher salt (plus more to taste)

Cranberry Almond Snack Bites

2 cups rolled oats

1 1/2 cups almond butter

1 cup dried cranberries

1/4 cup maple syrup

1 teaspoon ground cinnamon

1/4 cup wheat germ

1/4 teaspoon almond extract

1/4 teaspoon kosher salt (plus more to taste)

1. Choose which snack bite recipe you'd like to make. Then, in a large bowl, mix together all the ingredients for that version. Add additional salt to taste.
2. Form into 1 1/2-inch balls and line them up on a baking sheet. (Pro tip: Sometimes the dough can be a little easier to work with if you let the mixture sit for a few minutes after mixing, *then* shape the bites with slightly wet hands.) Move the baking sheet to the refrigerator and refrigerate the bites until hardened, about an hour.
3. Serve immediately, or transfer to a container and store in the refrigerator for about a week. Alternatively, you can keep the snack bites in an airtight container in the freezer for several months.

Notes: Instead of chocolate chips, you could use cacao nibs for a healthier version. In my opinion, the sweetness of the honey in the recipe is enough to compensate for the bitterness of the cacao nibs.

Wheat germ adds a bit of extra fiber and other nutrients, but feel free to use other ingredients like chia seeds or ground flaxseed, especially if you want to make these gluten-free.

18
Something Hallowed

CALLIE FEYEN

I am not here to convince the Presbyterian Church to use donuts in place of bread for Communion, but it's a good thing Do-Rite Donuts isn't in Ann Arbor. Because I'm certain that a task force, a prayer team, and some other committee would be formed to bring this idea to fruition, and no Presbyterian has time for another meeting.

It's just that these donuts are bring-you-to-your-knees, thank-the-Lord-for-sugar-and-a-fryer amazing. They come at you rolled in cinnamon and sugar, drizzled with chocolate or vanilla icing, doused in rainbow sprinkles, some with bacon on them. Like most donuts, they arrive in a box, but each one has its own square, something I find delightful *and* appetizing. I love designations and categories. I love assignments and to-do lists that are only mine to complete. I do not work well with others. The phrase *stay in your lane* could be my manifesto. Also, I do not share food.

One look at these donuts, and I feel seen—that's what I'm trying to say.

It was my brother, Geoff, who knew about the donuts and carried a box of them to a park nestled in the city of Chicago on the most brilliant autumn morning the Midwest could ever dream up.

This was Geoff's idea—the donuts and the park. We were in town for my mom and dad's fiftieth wedding anniversary, and he suggested we take the kids out and meet up with our uncle Greg and our oldest cousin, Todd. Geoff's good at stuff like that. You know, being kind. I was two when I spoke my first full sentences: "Don't talk to me. Don't even look at me." I fear these requests still hold true for me most days. I get so stressed about family dynamics and scheduling and making sure everyone is happy that I end up doing nothing. I'm so lucky to have Geoff as my brother. He drags me out of my lane and onto a much more vivid, albeit curvy, road.

We were at the park, the day bright and crisp. It was the kind of day that beckons movement, the sort that won't stand for folks simply standing in the light. Leaves scratched their way across the pavement, about as fast as the kids running around, their sweatshirts loose around their waists and slipping. I stood next to Uncle Greg, who brought his five-year-old grandson, Josiah, to play and eat donuts, too. Josiah calls Greg "Papa," which works well because in the span of about a year, Greg lost his daughter and then his wife. "Papa" fits for who he was and who he became.

Greg and I have never suffered small talk with each other. Even as a kid, he's always been the person I've been able to tell anything to. I don't mean stuff like what toys I want for Christmas or which boy I like. I mean *really* strange stuff, like how much I love to make plans and color code my belongings. Or that my dream job was and always will be some kind of hybrid professional shopper, organizer, decorator, librarian, and one of the girls who dance the halftime show at the Chicago Bulls basketball games. Greg always talks to me like everything I say makes sense, and we've never shied away from tough topics. So I felt strange that day since I was giving off small-talk vibes.

I was nervous though. A handful of weeks before, Greg had asked my husband, Jesse, and I if we would be godparents to Josiah, but I said no.

That morning, my no felt like a confession creeping over the wall of skyscrapers and breathing swirls of icy autumn from Lake Michigan's waves crashing on the shore beyond.

"It's okay," Greg told me as he took a donut. Then he told me about all the things being made new in his life: the teachers and the school his boy loves and is thriving in. The woman he's met. "I think I'm going to ask her to marry me," he told me, then took a bite of the chocolate-covered sour cream donut he was holding.

About then, my cousin Todd showed up with his wife, Monica. Todd and Monica lost a son earlier that year. His name was Noah. To know Todd is to know the sun personified. It is impossible not to feel bright around him. He is a prankster, he is hilarious, and he has the ability to bring out everyone's vivaciousness. He was no different on this day, and I worried that he felt he had to put on a show when his heart was breaking. Maybe it was the donuts we were sharing, but I soon forgot about everything he'd been through that year because I was laughing too hard at his quick wit.

After a while, Jesse walked over to a stand selling apples and bought some for all of us. I love my donuts, but there isn't anything better in autumn than the crisp crunch of an apple just plucked from a tree.

I love my donuts, but there isn't anything better in autumn than the crisp crunch of an apple just plucked from a tree.

In my family, we have a longstanding joke that if I were to pitch our collective story to a publisher, they'd say, "No way. That's too dramatic." Name the bad things, and they've either happened or we've done them: cancer, divorce, affairs, substance abuse, stealing. I think the only one of the Ten Commandments we haven't broken is murder. Our trouble started with my grandfather, my mom's dad. He was living in Egypt at the time and walking home with his friend after work. They were shot at. His friend was killed, and my grandfather knew that he was next. So he took his wife, my grandma, and his five- and six-year-old daughters and sweet-talked his way onto a boat none of them were supposed to be on. His lie is why we're all alive today, why we could eat apples and donuts and run around a park in the middle of a city as we suffered heartache on a picture-perfect autumn day.

There's a story in the Bible where John the Baptist tells the crowds listening to him that things were about to change because Someone was coming who was going to change everything. The crowd takes in his words and responds with, essentially, "Well, what should we do, John?" Three times, different folks in the crowd ask him this question, and three times John responds with the same basic message: "Care for one another. Give all that you have, and don't take more than you need. Take care of each other."

> **What I believe, what I am a witness to, is that we can be broken beyond belief and that here in the depths is where hope takes root.**

I often wish I was the kind of person who's a little friendlier, a little more generous. I wish I didn't startle and get overwhelmed as easily as I do. I wish I didn't do—or want to do—bad things. *But here I am,* I thought, *standing with my brother and my family, sharing in some kind of strange and hallowed Communion. Here I am, loved more than I'll ever comprehend. Here are all of us—the shattered and the shattering—trying to bring forth hope.*

I do not think that everything will be okay. I do not believe we will all live happily ever after. What I believe, what I am a witness to, is that we can be broken beyond belief and that here in the depths is where hope takes root. This is as true as the leaves that gasp out the colors of fire before they fall to the ground. This is the dark mystery I cling to.

That day, we all kept talking while our kids kept playing. My brother reached for another donut, broke it in half, and offered it to me. Like I said, I don't share food. But I shared—and will keep sharing—in that.

Lazy Weekend Donuts

I wish I could give each reader their own box of Do-Rite Donuts, but alas, I do not have the skill of Martha Stewart. What I do have, though, is a donut recipe that is easy to make and equally delicious. Your weekend brunch game will thank me.

MAKES 8 DONUTS AND 8 DONUT HOLES

3/4 cup vegetable oil, divided
1 (8-count) package large refrigerated biscuits
1/2 cup granulated sugar
1/4 teaspoon ground cinnamon

Note: This recipe is adapted from *Real Simple* magazine's May 2007 issue.

1. In a medium skillet, warm 1/2 cup of the oil on medium-low heat.
2. While the oil heats, place the biscuit dough on a cutting board. Using a 1-inch-round cookie or biscuit cutter, cut and remove a hole from the center of each piece of dough. (Pro tip: Keep the dough centers to make donut holes!)
3. In a single layer, place the donuts in the skillet, and cook for about 90 seconds. Flip and repeat the process for the other side, frying until golden brown and cooked through.
4. Transfer donuts to a wire rack or a paper towel-lined plate.
5. Repeat this process until all donuts and donut holes are cooked, adding more oil to the skillet along the way as needed.
6. In a medium bowl, combine the sugar and cinnamon. Gently toss the warm donuts in the mixture, and serve immediately.

19

Cocoon

BECKY MORQUECHO

My laptop bag, yoga mat, and leather tote are piled by the front door, my makeup is fresh, and my sunglasses and keys are in hand.

"Mama, do you *have* to go?" my eight-year-old daughter pleads.

She initiates a hug, burying her head in my ribs. I squish my cheek into her shiny dark hair, inhaling the lingering lavender from last night's bath. Her perfect almond-shaped eyes look straight into mine when I tell her how much I love her. When I tell her to giggle with her friends, there are no tears, only the beautiful reality that we'll miss each other.

Yes, I need to go.

I pull up a bumpy gravel driveway to my friend Chelsea's house, open the driver's side door, and step out into the late summer air, thick with humidity and possibility.

I grab the paper grocery bag full of goodies—our favorite hummus, salted dark chocolate, and red wine—and the potted Blackfoot Daisy I picked up earlier in the week at a local nursery.

My friend walks out to greet me, and together we unload the rest of the bags from the back seat. Soon after, we begin a different kind of unpacking over a California red poured into what were once glass yogurt jars. I sit on a stool, my hands loosely folded on her counter, while Chels stands on the other side of the sleek, speckled surface, sipping her wine and spilling hard truths. I nod and listen, acknowledging and absorbing my friend's words. Then she redirects the question and opens the space between us.

After an initial catch-up, we realize we're starving not only for these conversations, but also for something to fill our bellies. Chels stirs Trader Joe's bruschetta mix, lentils, and feta in a silver metal bowl. We spoon it onto bite-size slices of French bread and devour it all. The next twenty minutes are a dance. Steam rising from the rice sweltering on the stove, swirling together with the aroma of garlic and lemon. Fears and laughter alike releasing from our lungs into the brimming kitchen air, then drifting out the screened window above the sink, an offering scattered into the wild.

We sit across from each another at her well-loved wooden table and eat our chicken shawarma bowls slowly but deliberately. At any other retreat, we'd be wearing our matching buttery black Vuori joggers, ready for an evening work session, followed by indulging in dark chocolate and a splash of wine—the communion of friendship—and belly laughing on the couch watching stand-up comedians on Netflix. But tonight we move with more purpose because tonight we have somewhere to go.

Our adoption agency told us to "cocoon" when we arrived home from China as a family of three. Stay home. Don't let anyone else feed, bathe, or comfort your child, they said. And we listened. Our brave baby—twenty months old when we met her—left everything she knew and was handed to two eager strangers. It only made sense that we'd try to ease her grief with as much love and consistency as possible.

For the first couple months, the three of us enmeshed our voices, our scents, our preferences, our sleep, our laughs, our cries, our affection. We blended it all together in hopes of creating security for our girl, along with attachment and soothed nervous systems—among the inherent brokenness of adoption—for us all. We clung to each other, snug and safe from any outliers that didn't weave us together tighter. I held my daughter as close as I could. Never wanting to let go.

Two years into motherhood, I stood in our dimly lit kitchen scrubbing dishes, desperate for post-bedtime relief to slow the pumping of my heart and calm the incessant thoughts bombarding my frazzled nerves. *I need to get out of here, but I can't leave,* I convinced myself. I had begged and waited for my daughter, but the reality was that my delight and joy were often matched with overwhelm and suffocation, like bricks being tied to my ankles as I helplessly sank into the depths of the sea.

Something happens to a woman when she goes from being childless to feeding, rocking, shushing, holding, changing, distracting, delighting in, worrying about, and fearing for someone else.

She grows in holy love, yes. But sometimes she slowly drowns.

I needed something for myself. But I was too afraid to leave the shelter of our hard-won attachment, too afraid to disrupt the cocoon of trust built around us.

Five years ago, on a whim, I texted Chelsea a link to a dreamy Airbnb. A getaway for the two of us. A respite from the demands of motherhood. Anxiety gnawed at my efforts: Would that hard-won attachment with my daughter withstand my leaving? I only hoped. But could I be the mother she needed me to be if I stayed? No.

When I stepped inside that urban bungalow for our first retreat, space and silence cushioned me like cumulus clouds. Afternoon rays poured through the sheer curtains and danced on the signature millennial white walls. A thriving pothos plant dangled its vines down from a corner of the ceiling. *If I absorb the light and space of this place, can I flourish again, too?* I wondered.

We constructed a charcuterie board of sugar-dusted almonds, rich salami, Brie, and white cheddar. Cucumbers for crunch and color. Peaches and berries for summer sweetness. We spread before us a buffet of note-books, ideas, and art waiting to be made. We fed ourselves grown-up snacks and bright opportunities. And at the end of the night, we slathered clay on our faces, painted our nails, and watched anything that made us laugh.

As I returned home from that first retreat, my deep-seated fears clapped and jeered. My sweet girl's mind had instinctually instructed her to stiff-arm my love. I was desperate to look into her eyes, to make a case for myself, to remind her of the closeness we shared. But it took a week of dripping love and affection, diluting the hurt of her triggered system. A week of hunkering down, wrapping my arms and our walls around her.

Still, as hard as it was to leave my daughter, Chels and I continued our ritual of creating a sacred, safe space for ourselves and each other twice a year. A tiny—yet expansive—pocket of nourishment, hidden away from the world. A place to look inward, grow, and become.

At one retreat in particular, at the end of a productive day of creative projects, I walked into Chelsea's kitchen to offer help with dinner.

"What can I do?" I asked.

But to my surprise, Chels said dinner was almost finished. The chicken thighs had been soaking up the honey, orange juice, and coconut aminos all day in the Crock-Pot. They were tender and ready to be shredded. Chels simmered and thickened the sauce, the flame of the stove crackling the bottom of the pan.

So I sat at the dining table, on the wooden bench closest to the west-facing window. The warm winter light and her kindness swallowed me whole, and I let them.

A few minutes later, my friend—who also needed time to deflate her worries, revel in silence, and fill up her cup—heaped a hearty serving of thoughtfulness in the form of cabbage salad bathed in oil and vinegar and topped with slivered almonds, jasmine rice, and sesame-orange chicken onto my plate.

I couldn't recall the last time someone cooked real, delicious, mouth-watering food for me. It felt like a fairy tale. An overflowing well.

Chels and I stack our plates that are smeared with hummus and dotted with oregano in the sink and head toward separate bathrooms to get ready for the night. As I'm applying mascara, wearing my black two-piece linen set, I hear Chels's footsteps rounding the corner. One glance at each other and we collapse into laughter.

We're wearing the *exact* same thing.

I'm not surprised.

I met Chelsea in 2009, the same year we both got married. She and my husband first met when they were only four years old at her cousin's fire truck birthday party. I always tell people that when Jesse introduced me to Chelsea, I decided right away: *Yes, I'll take her, too, please.*

My friendship with Chels grew easily, with our mutual love of thrift-ing and making art. She begged God beside me for our daughter to come home. And right before we left for China to meet that daughter, Chelsea perfectly styled my baby shower, making my only request come alive: an array of fuchsia bougainvillea and cutie tangerines. Color and life.

Chelsea is the girl who makes everything beautiful. Nooks, tabletops, experiences, and feelings, all begging to be noticed. She finds and creates beauty without effort, not in vain, but rather to make you feel worthy and welcome. Together, we have endured loss, grief, and depression. Yet we always find our way back to warmth, beauty, and laughter. And apparently, a mutual love of black linen.

Still laughing, Chels walks back to her bedroom closet. Eventually, she lands on a black linen romper. Our outfits seem different enough as we walk out the door, but in the end—when we're both wearing denim jackets—we still end up looking like twins.

In those early years of motherhood, once my daughter and I had cemented our bond, I was so afraid to lose what we'd built. I was so afraid to leave her. So afraid to stretch the silk that had given us the space to cultivate our own unique love and family. Terrified that the strings would snap and be irreparable.

Growth is a part of the process of living. Cocoons are only temporary.

But I'm learning that my job as a mother—even an adoptive mother who was encouraged to Bubble Wrap her family at first—is not to shield my daughter, or our relationship, indefinitely from the hurts of this world. Growth is a part of the process of living. Cocoons are only temporary.

—•⟫⟪•—

Our phones flash with a group text from our husbands. It's a photo of our three girls—two of them eight, one ten, mouths full of grown-up teeth—wearing colorful cotton summer jammies, hugging our fluffy pup. The girls' smiles are the brightest light in our kitchen. My daughter is embracing her friends, a feat that's taken years of practice for a little girl who's rightfully been hesitant to find freedom in all-encompassing love. I quickly reply to Jesse, *Vera looks so happy!*

A burly man wearing a straight face and slicked-back hair interrupts my bliss and demands that everyone please put their phones away. The comedian Chels and I have been watching on Netflix for years enters the arena, and the crowd whistles and hollers as the music and my adrenaline *thump, thump, thump.* I feel free from responsibility. Free from the prison of anxiety about stepping away from motherhood for a night or two. Free to be a woman out in the world splurging on tickets and laughter and friendship.

Chels and I grasp each other's hands, bellowing shrieks, hyperventilating, our cheek muscles in slaphappy pain for an hour. She breaks off a piece of the excessively salty concession stand soft pretzel and passes me the remains. We wash it down with one shared cup of overpriced water. No dark chocolate. No wine. But Communion nonetheless.

In the morning, we'll get back to our joggers, our projects, our cocoon. I'll get back to writing about what moves me most: motherhood and reclaiming who I am outside of it. But tonight is a celebration, a culmination of weekends away, memories, meals, and taking time to care for each other.

Time to see and be ourselves, away from—but also as an example *for*—our daughters.

Slow Cooker Sesame-Orange Chicken

Since the first time Chelsea made this dish for me, the ingredients have been a permanent staple on my grocery list. Just the other day, as I flipped to the recipe page in my worn copy of Danielle Walker's Against All Grain *cookbook, my daughter commented, "You* really *like making this." It's true. This is hands-down one of the easiest, most delicious meals you can make for yourself and others. We serve this chicken over jasmine rice and often have a cabbage salad on the side.*

MAKES 4 SERVINGS

2 pounds boneless, skinless chicken thighs
1/3 cup coconut aminos
1/3 cup honey
2 tablespoons orange juice
2 tablespoons tomato paste
1 tablespoon toasted sesame oil
2 garlic cloves, minced
1/2 teaspoon ground ginger
3/4 teaspoon kosher salt
1/2 teaspoon red pepper flakes
1/4 teaspoon black pepper
Sesame seeds and green onions, chopped, for garnish
4 cups cooked rice

1. In a large slow cooker at least 6 quarts in size, place the chicken thighs in a single layer.
2. In a medium bowl, whisk together the coconut aminos, honey, orange juice, tomato paste, sesame oil, garlic, ginger, salt, red pepper flakes, and black pepper. Pour the sauce over the chicken. Turn the chicken to ensure it's evenly coated in the sauce.
3. Place the lid on the slow cooker and cook on low for 4 hours, or until the meat reaches an internal temperature of 165 degrees.
4. Remove the chicken from the sauce, place on a cutting board, and cut into bite-size cubes.
5. Using a spoon, remove any fat from the top of the sauce, then transfer the sauce to a

small saucepan. Simmer the sauce over medium heat for 20 minutes, or until the sauce has reduced by half and is thick and shiny. Add the chicken to the sauce and toss until the meat is fully coated.

6. Serve warm over rice, and garnish with sesame seeds and green onions.

Notes: This recipe is adapted from Danielle Walker's *Against All Grain* cookbook.[1]

If you don't have coconut aminos, you can substitute soy sauce for similar results.

20

With Limón and Salt

NEIDY HESS

I grew up in Atlanta, Georgia, in a tiny apartment with a single Mexican mom and my siblings. My friends who lived in the suburbs grew up among wealth: They knew summers with lemonade stands on the corners of their neighborhoods, right by the well-manicured golf courses and tennis courts where they received private lessons. But I lived in a different part of town, where I shared a room with my oldest sister, and I'd hear the *paletero*, a Latino ice cream man, ring his bell while he walked by with lime Popsicles and well-dressed elotes.

I knew my home was different from my friends' homes, so I was nervous to have anyone over. Still, I worked up the courage to invite a new friend over for popsicles. She said yes, and I welcomed her into my space, praying she would approve of the *paletas* from my favorite *paletero*. Standing in my kitchen, she noticed one of the drawers was cracked open. Inside were all our limes.

"Wow, does your mom make a lot of key lime pie?"

"Huh?" I asked.

"You know—pie? A key lime one with whipped cream on top?"

I had no idea what she was talking about and met her awed face with confusion. *Limes in a pie? What's a pie?*

But I said nothing. I didn't want to risk needing to explain how different we were and risk my new friend not wanting to spend time with me anymore.

There's a saying in Spanish: *Take hard things with limón y sal* (lime and salt). Ultimately, you take the bitter parts to pucker up for the sour parts and enjoy the tang. The risk is worth the flavor.

When I first heard the saying, *When life gives you lemons, make lemonade*, I was so unfamiliar with lemons that I mistook it to mean something like, *When life hands you something marvelous, make the most of it.* To me, lemons represented a bright, sparkling hope—fully symbolizing true-blue Americana and entrepreneurial dreams. Lemons were synonymous with silver spoons. That's why I thought all bright and shiny neighborhoods had lemonade stands dotting every corner.

I grew up with limes in kitchen drawers. Normal and ordinary, limes were better suited for living among plastic cutlery and tinfoil and canned pickled jalapeños and for street tacos sold by an aunt or uncle.

To my family and me, limes were commonplace, not at all exotic. Every recipe that needed a tiny bit of flavor or seasoning required limes. Salsa? Add a squeeze of lime. Poultry? Rub a lime on it. A glass of Coke? More lime. Limes belonged in the boiling-hot kitchen with wafts of spicy chilies that would choke out the oxygen and burn your eyes. Limes laced those flavors of my childhood.

I would squeeze every little bit out of my lime on my pozole or tacos because, while they were ordinary, I still enjoyed how limes brightened up the food on my plate. Even so, I would daydream about eating my lime-saturated esquites, a corn salad, alongside a glass of cold lemonade.

Could I admit that I liked both?

Eventually, I grew up. I moved out of my mom's tiny apartment and got married. My husband and I made San Diego our home while my husband served in the military, but we never put down roots. Once his military service ended, we got to choose our next home—in Iowa. We moved to a little town where I pictured a lemonade stand on the corner down the block from our little blue house—a slice of Americana just for me. We began to attend a local community church, and our kids started at a small school in town. It was what I thought life ought to be—Friday night lights among cornfields, festivals in the church parking lot under the monumental eggshell steeple, and our babysitter bagging my groceries at the grocery store where she worked during the week.

I loved this new place. Being an extrovert, I wanted to get to know my neighbors and new friends, so when a job at a church opened up, I applied and was welcomed in.

I served with a woman whose children were the same age as mine. Our spouses both worked in service-oriented careers, and our similarities allowed us to initiate a conversation with fewer questions and more laughter. Our bond with one another grew.

But when we served together, we looked like a pair of mismatched socks. Her slick golden hair contrasted against my dark, thick curls. She grew up with a lemonade stand in her neighborhood, and I grew up with limes in kitchen drawers. Even as we served together, I wondered if we could ever be friends.

Occasionally, she would say something about "those people in the city" or make a face when I described squeezing lime wedges into my favorite dishes like menudo or lengua tacos, foods unfamiliar to her. Something in me bristled when this happened, but I would quickly dismiss these infrequent comments. We had other things in common, and we didn't need to completely understand one another.

One Sunday, I stood with my clipboard to greet families as they entered the children's wing of our church. I noticed an older woman, a visitor, moving a table that belonged to the children's area. Noticing the small mistake, I interrupted her.

"I'm so sorry, but we need this table here. We use it to display our children's materials on Sundays."

Her kind face turned into a scowl. With disdain, she informed me—no, she *berated* me—I had no jurisdiction over the table. As she spoke, my heart began to race. Heat rushed to my face, and I held down tears of humiliation while she shouted at me as if I were a defiant little girl. While the woman belittled me, my new friend stood back and said nothing.

Her silence was deafening.

The older woman huffed away, saying she would talk to my pastor, my boss. I swallowed my salty tears and hid behind my clipboard for a moment. I cleared my throat, welcomed the next family, and signed their child in for Sunday's programming. Once I cleaned up all the materials from the activities, I got in my car, drove home, and cried until I parked in my garage.

A week after the experience, I attempted to talk with my friend about the woman's comment. "She didn't mean that," she'd said. "She's much too nice of an old lady." She didn't see the hurt the way I felt it. And her dismissal stung. I didn't yet know that this would foreshadow more miscommunication and other missteps after I'd try to confide deep hurts to her. Each time, she remained silent.

As much as I wanted to be close, I realized we couldn't be friends if she didn't recognize how I, as an immigrant's daughter with dark skin and dark eyes who spoke a different first language, saw and experienced the world.

Our friendship soured and never recovered.

A few years later, my family and I waved goodbye to the small town in cornfields and moved to a home in the inner suburbs of Omaha. Our kids pass tennis courts on their way to school, but we can also grab Popsicles with Tajín just a few minutes away. Our house has a place in the kitchen, right under the cabinets, with space for where I keep my favorite bowl. I fill it with limes *and* lemons.

Soon after we moved in, we invited a family from church over. The wife sang in front of our congregation while her husband played the drums. Their children were in the same stage as our two older ones. Because of my apprehension in wanting to make new friends, I tidied my house in preparation for our guests, my mind spiraling with anxiety. *Will my youngest feel left out of the group? Will they think we're weird? Will she even be my friend?*

After the initial small talk at our front door, we walked toward our living room. We asked each other about our families, where we grew up, and how long we'd each lived in Omaha. Our little conversation felt a lot like dipping our toes in a pool for the first time.

Our kids showed similar hesitation until my daughter invited our new friends' daughter for a snack. I watched the little girl walk into our kitchen. She stopped to look at my cookbooks on the counter, touched our striped kitchen towel, and tapped her fingers on the counter, but she paused in front of my favorite bowl.

"Oh my gosh—you have *lemons*?" she squealed. "My mom never buys these. They're way too nice."

The question made me laugh, and whatever fears I held inside were released. A year later, Lacey's family and mine continued to get to know each other. As moms, we joke about the ridiculous things our kids say, and we feel safe enough to complain to one another when parenting gets hard. Our children equally complain to each another about how annoying their moms can be when we make them do chores. Lacey's children

Finding a friend who cherishes every little bit of your worldview, no matter how different you are from one another, is a bright, shiny gift.

also ask me how to pronounce words in Spanish while mine ask Lacey how to play her favorite board games. But what solidified our friendship more than anything was when I came to her grieving a bitter pain. She didn't dismiss it. She listened. In time, she also offered me the opportunity to hold her sorrows, and I was grateful to do so.

For my birthday last year, Lacey got me daisies with fake lemons hanging off the side. She said she wanted to give me a bougie gift. And somehow, that made us both laugh until we cried.

Finding a friend who cherishes every little bit of your worldview, no matter how different you are from one another, is a bright, shiny gift. And like lemons, you make the most of it. And like limes, something beautiful can come out of the ordinary.

Corn Cucumber Citrus Salad

This salad is another take on a Mexican street food called esquites *(pronounced es-KEE-tehs). The lemon-lime twist infuses sweetness and a bitterness with each bite. It's intended to be every bit refreshing—and never intended to be enjoyed alone. Be sure to bring this side for your next lunch or dinner date with a friend.*

MAKES 8 SERVINGS

For the salad

2 cups frozen corn
1 splash water
1 tablespoon avocado or vegetable oil
1 cup cucumber, seeded or unseeded, with skin, chopped
1 jalapeño, seeded and diced
Fresh cilantro to taste, chopped

For the salad

1. In a medium bowl, pour in the corn with a splash of water, and microwave for about 1 minute, or until thawed.
2. In a medium skillet, pour in the oil and turn the heat to medium-high. Add the thawed corn to the skillet and stir until some corn kernels are seared and browned, about 5 minutes. Remove the skillet from heat, place the corn in a medium bowl, and place the bowl in the refrigerator for about 20 minutes.
3. After the corn cools, add the chopped cucumber and jalapeño, and set aside.

For the dressing

Juice from 1 lemon

Juice from 1 lime

1 tablespoon avocado or olive oil

2 teaspoon Tajín or chili lime seasoning

1/2 teaspoon cayenne pepper

1/4 teaspoon paprika

2/3 cup mayonnaise

Pinch of salt to taste

2/3 cup crumbled cotija cheese or grated Parmesan cheese

Cilantro, chopped, for garnish, optional

For the dressing

1. Combine the lemon juice, lime juice, oil, Tajín, cayenne pepper, paprika, mayonnaise, and salt. Whisk vigorously for 30 seconds. Add cotija and continue to whisk for another minute, until the dressing is combined.
2. To dress the salad, drizzle 1/3 of the salad dressing on top of the corn mixture, and toss to combine. Drizzle the remaining dressing to taste and toss. Garnish with cilantro, if using, then serve.

21

Same Script, Different Cast

ADRIENNE GARRISON

My favorite holiday tradition as a child was our annual trip to Chicago for a Christmas gathering with extended family. It felt as though all the season's anticipation and festivity had been leading to this moment when we all gathered at my grandfather's small suburban cottage. I loved being surrounded by aunts, uncles, big cousins, and little cousins. I loved weaving through legs to observe as they cooked, played cards, watched football, or sang along with Auntie Gayle as she played carols on the piano.

A high point of our celebration was Aunt Betty's arrival with her basket of cookies. Nestled into a bed of green and red cellophane were buttery spritz cookies in the shape of poinsettias and wreaths, sugar cookies dusted with sprinkles that crackled between your teeth, and snowball cookies rolled in powdered sugar that left us all begging for glasses of milk. There were cookies twisted and shaped to look like candy canes, spicy gingerbread men, and thumbprint cookies filled with raspberry jam. Oh, how we waited and waited for that front door to open, for Aunt Betty to come through in her wool dress coat and smart little hat, the large wicker basket of cookies filling her arms! And that is how it came to be that, for me, it wasn't really Christmas unless there were cookies.

Years later, as a new bride, my husband and I relocated to Chicago for graduate school. His studies were especially demanding, and by the time the holidays rolled around, I was insatiably lonely whether he was across the couch or across the city. I wondered which of my brand-new friends might invite me to a glitzy, glamorous New Year's Eve party or to go ice skating downtown after visiting the Christkindlmarket. In the movies, the twenty-something young woman in the city was always popping in and out of gatherings. I longed to be in the middle of something festive and bustling, like my childhood Christmases. So instead of sitting around waiting until a gathering magically appeared, I printed some invitations and passed them out to fellow teachers at the preschool where I taught, to friends from grad school, and to one or two of my husband's female classmates. It was a disparate group, to be sure, but I felt this might be an asset for the gathering I had in mind. In December 2009, I held my very first cookie exchange.

> **Flinging the door of my apartment open wide with the promise of cookies was a wild gamble, a fierce hope that even after the party was over, a few of these women might stick around in my day-to-day life.**

The instructions were simple enough: Bring three dozen of your favorite Christmas cookies and return home with thirty-six cookies of every sort. As the guests walked out of my apartment that year, everyone looked like Aunt Betty carrying piles of treats. My contribution had been to roll, cut, and bake heaps of sugar cookies for my guests to decorate and take home. To some, I may have seemed like "the hostess with the mostest." But in truth, this was hospitality as a defense mechanism. Flinging the door of my apartment open wide with the promise of cookies was a wild gamble, a fierce hope that even after the party was over, a few of these women might stick around in my day-to-day life.

The following year, we moved a few neighborhoods away into what became my favorite apartment. Our third-floor attic remodel in Lincoln Square was never cozier than when it was filled with friends old and new, all of them passing out cookies they'd lovingly created in their own kitchens. I realized my guests needed some sustenance to counter all the sweets, so I looked for a recipe that felt both healthy and decadent, a curried butternut squash soup that I've tweaked and served nearly every year since.

By year three, I had the rhythm down. Our little apartment was lined with friends from every era of my life—a friend from high school visiting the city, coworkers from the elementary school where I worked, dear friends from grad school, and friends my husband and I had made together. They came, they ate, and they left with smorgasbords of sugary treats. The simple ingredients of the gathering allowed me to focus on deepening my friendships and enjoying the moment.

Then we moved to California, and I felt like we were starting over. Loneliness followed me everywhere as I adjusted to a warm winter holiday while my family was thousands of miles away. I couldn't break through the surface-level, getting-to-know-you chitchat with the new people I met. As lovely as they were, no one seemed to want to connect beyond initial introductions. Their social spheres were complete. My only hope was to lean into the key lesson I had learned in my early twenties: You can't be left out of a party you host yourself.

I didn't know anyone, but I had mastered the art of hosting a dang good cookie party, so I channeled my inner Aunt Betty and set to work with invitations as November turned into December. For my fourth annual cookie swap, my husband's coworker Alicia brought impossibly fluffy homemade marshmallows. At the fifth exchange, my teaching partner, Lauren, introduced me to brown-butter Rice Krispies treats. In the sixth year, I could truly say that Mariah, whose husband was in training with mine, made the world's most delicious sugar cookies (and by then I was a bit of a connoisseur). In my new city, I was grateful to have the comfort of this tradition to fall back on, where acquaintances might blossom into full-fledged friendships.

It takes time to build community. In these years of frequent moves, I realized it took about two and a half years to feel I had truly close friends. Given that we were moving every four years, this meant the last cookie party in our "new" hometown was the most meaningful. This was why I decided, just three weeks postpartum with my first baby, that I couldn't skip out on the seventh annual cookie exchange. After all, it was our last Christmas in California. This is also why, three years later, after relocating my family and my tradition back to the Midwest, I determined it was still absolutely necessary for me to have the cookie swap just a few days after we'd moved into a new house. The structure made it feel okay to continue to gather women from the four corners of my life, no matter where I lived. Same script, different cast.

But a global pandemic and a third baby were enough to bring my annual cookie swap to a screeching halt. There was no twelfth cookie exchange and no thirteenth either. I barely had the chance to grieve this loss amid so many unknowns. When things came back online, I couldn't get excited about the cookie party again. When the calendar turned over to December 2023, I still hadn't sent out a single invitation. On one hand, I grieved the loss of this cherished holiday get-together. On the other hand, at thirty-six years old, I was lucky enough to be rich in friendships. My original motivation was never to stock up on enough cookies to last me well into the new year, but to find my people.

When I decided against the party again, I didn't realize anyone might notice. Then I received a text from my sweet friend Marci: *Do you think you'll have the cookie exchange this year?*

Honestly, I don't think so, I texted back. *I can barely gather the energy to make a meal or tidy my house from day to day, let alone get things together for a party.*

That makes sense, she replied. But I could tell she'd been counting on that opportunity to share the holiday magic with friends, to be in the middle of a wonderful, warm, buzzing gathering of women. She'd moved into our neighborhood a few months into the pandemic and had found it difficult to meet people.

Maybe the cookie swap could live on. Perhaps it was time to keep the cast, but change the script a bit.

Any chance you'd be willing to host? I texted back. *I'll make the invitations and pass them around to our neighbors if we can have it at your house! I'll even bring the soup!*

Marci loved that idea, and so my annual cookie swap got a new home, a new host, and (as always) new recipes. This December we will gather in her living room once again with holiday tunes playing in the background and cookies covering every available surface. As conversation and laughter fill the room, I'll feel the sense of connection I've always longed for at Christmas. And like every year, I will think of my Aunt Betty as friends old and new bundle up against the winter wind and carefully carry their trays full of treats home to their own families.

Curried Butternut Squash Soup

Who doesn't love the warm, welcoming smell of soup greeting them at the door? The bit of curry in this recipe is mostly aromatic and definitely isn't spicy. I know the combination of sautéed apples with onion may seem strange, but trust *me. This is just the cozy, decadent meal that your guests need to balance out all those cookies.*

MAKES 8 SERVINGS

- 1 butternut squash, about 2 1/2 pounds
- 2 tablespoons olive oil
- 2 tablespoons butter
- 3 medium sweet yellow onions, diced
- 2 large Honeycrisp apples, peeled and cut into 1-inch cubes
- 1/4 cup firmly packed brown sugar
- 1 1/2 tablespoons curry powder
- 6 cups chicken or vegetable stock
- 1 (8-ounce) container mascarpone cheese
- 2 teaspoons salt

1. Preheat the oven to 375 degrees. Line a baking sheet with foil.
2. Cut the butternut squash in half lengthwise, and remove the seeds and stringy bits. Brush the cut surface with olive oil, and place cut-side down on a baking sheet. Roast for about 40 minutes, or until fork-tender.
3. While the squash is roasting, melt the butter in a Dutch oven or large stock pot over medium heat. Add the onions and cook for 5 to 6 minutes or until tender, stirring occasionally.
4. Add the apples, brown sugar, and curry powder. Cook for about 1 minute, stirring constantly, until curry powder is fragrant. Add the stock and bring to a simmer over medium heat. Cover the soup and let it simmer for an additional 24 to 26 minutes. Remove from heat.

5. When the squash is done roasting, let it cool for a few minutes, then scoop the flesh out of the skin. Carefully add the roasted squash to the soup, and use an immersion blender to blend the soup until smooth.
6. Add the mascarpone and salt to the soup, and whisk until the mascarpone is fully incorporated. Bring the soup to a simmer over medium heat. Let the soup simmer for 2 minutes and then remove from the heat.
7. Serve with crusty bread and a hearty salad.

Notes: This recipe is adapted from The Pampered Chef.[1]

If you don't have an immersion blender, carefully ladle about 1/3 of the soup into a regular blender. Cover and blend until smooth, and repeat with the remaining soup. When all the soup is blended, return the soup to the cooking pot and proceed with step 6.

22

Just Be There with Me

SONYA SPILLMANN

The text is unexpected, as any death announcement would be.

I can't believe I'm writing this, my best friend Stacey had typed. *My dad passed away last night.* Her dad, the man with the best laugh in the world. Her dad, with the eyes that twinkled in the moments right before a perfectly timed punch line. Her dad, the one who I knew, with one look, loved her more than life.

An ache—no, something more like an emptied-outness—fills my core.

I'm sorry to text this to you, she writes next.

I read, then reread her words. The news can't be real. Of course it's not real. My throat tightens and my arms feel like they might disintegrate. My heart does not start to beat wildly, but my breathing changes and my body is no longer connected to the ground.

It is real.

Of course it's real.

I frantically text our group of friends from high school: *We have to send food / I need to do something / What can we do?*

Another friend will call—to check in on *me.* "Are you okay?" she will ask, and I will burst into tears.

"It's just that," I'll try to explain, "when *my* mom died . . ." Did I finish my sentence? Did I have to explain?

It will take me another few days to understand what I experienced in my mind and body during those hours. How, after that text, I time-traveled back to age eighteen. I wasn't feeling lost and hopeless, more like swirling in an abyss of the unknown.

A tsunami of memory had leveled me.

Stacey and I met on the first day of fourth grade. As I recall, she sat in front of me, whipped her chestnut brown hair around, smiled the same smile she has as a grown woman—kind and somewhat mischievous—and said, "Hi, I'm Stacey, I'm new." I was new, too, and through the coming days, months, and years, we'd orbit around each other like twin planets, bound together with a force as constant as gravity.

I grew up in a strict Christian family belonging to a denomination that, among the traditions of women covering their heads and not wearing jewelry, did not allow dating or dancing. We were also encouraged not to have friends outside of church. Meaning that school friends were exactly that—*for* and *kept to* the hours during which we were at school. But Stacey and I became real friends, or at least we wanted to be. Friends who were dropped off at each other's houses and ate the snacks our moms bought and prank-called boys and complained about teachers and confessed crushes while lying on each other's comforters, staring up at the ceiling.

Stacey was, and still is, Jewish. And while this might have seemed problematic for a girl who wasn't even allowed to go to other Christian churches, it's as if Stacey's religion was a language my parents understood—one of faith and tradition, obligation and obedience. And so our friendship was called blessed.

We ran track together in middle school and swam countless laps in the same lane in high school. During the summers when she left for sleepaway camp, I went to church camp. And every fall we'd reunite, sharing stories of the boys we met, swapping clothing and secrets. We were the type of friends who passed notes during class, even though we'd walked in and would soon walk out together, so urgent was our need to connect. And though my parents didn't know my whole group of friends at school, I was allowed to go almost anywhere—minus dances—as long as Stacey was there.

Before our senior year of high school, I told Stacey how serious I was about the boy I liked. And also that my mom hadn't been feeling well. She told me about her summer adventures and all the fun she had as a counselor at camp. In the coming months, we applied to colleges. She would be going out of state; I'd be staying closer to home. We were co-captains on the swim team, in the water each morning by six. And although we knew our whole lives were still ahead of us, we didn't think too far beyond what the next year would bring.

After months of carrying a bottle of Tylenol under her arm and writing so many "I'll be home after my doctor's appointment" notes, my mom was diagnosed with cancer in the middle of March. *Cancer*. That's all we knew. That's all my brother, sister, and I were told. What power that one word can hold.

And what happens when no one looks you in the eye and says, "This is serious"? When no one tells you to "Pay attention," because someday soon you may not hear her voice, her laugh, or be able to feel the warmth of her hand. Was it magical thinking that made me assume she'd be fine? Or was it that since I was eighteen, I assumed—I *expected*—my parents would talk to me, tell me, treat me like an adult if it were the kind of cancer she would not survive?

Though food and people flooded our home, silence engulfed it in

> **Though food and people flooded our home, silence engulfed it in equal proportion.**

equal proportion. Whispers filled the rooms, but only until I walked in. My mom's weight dropped with each passing day, and the time she spent on the couch sleeping or staring at the birds grew longer.

It was Stacey to whom I first confessed the awful truth I had realized on Mother's Day—my mom was dying—and this would be the last one we'd share together. And it was Stacey I sat next to during an awards ceremony, four days before our high school graduation, when I saw my aunt rush down the darkened auditorium aisle. It was Stacey's knees I crawled over to follow my aunt out of the auditorium, trying to keep pace, and asked, "Did she . . . ?" unable able to say the words.

With tears in her eyes, my aunt nodded. She drove me back to the hospice facility. I walked down the hall to where my mother's lifeless body lay. I hugged my dad, both of us desperate with disbelief. Then I walked out the door, down a path, to the privacy of a man-made pond. While my younger brother and sister ran around nearby, trying to fly a kite, I lay myself out on a rock and cried. For how long I don't know—but then Stacey appeared.

She stood above me, and without words she handed me a white paper bag. I leaned forward, face swollen, heartbroken, and opened up her offering: an order of fried mushrooms and a burger wrapped in foil. I inhaled the scent of the familiar greasy food. What a strange, painful comfort.

In silence, with tears streaming down my face, I bit into the hot burger, letting every flavor linger on my tongue. The juicy flesh under the crispy mushrooms—a choice I normally would not have picked—was a taste I'll remember for the rest of my life. It was compassion, comfort, love.

Stacey sat there with me, our version of sitting shiva, until I was ready to talk.

In the wake of her dad's passing, twenty-eight years after my mom's, I stare at my phone in disbelief. Life can change in a minute. A second. A heartbeat. A breath. And maybe this is why my friendship with Stacey, this constant that has so often felt like it has held me together when so much of life has changed, is uniquely precious.

I want to be for her now what she was for me then—present, constant, like family. I call off work. Arrange carpool rides for my kids. Then drive to the bakery down the street. The woman behind the counter tells me which cake will travel the six hours best.

"Put it in a cooler," she says. "It'll be fine." I don't think it was Stacey's dad's favorite flavor, or even hers. But I know it doesn't matter—the important part is presence. Just bring something.

Anything.

I learned this lesson from her.

Stacey and I are not eighteen years old anymore. We are grown women, with daughters the same ages as we were then. We continue to live our lives in orbit of one another, still sharing joys and secrets, fears and confessions, birthdays and tears. We've taken vacations together and hopped on planes to connect.

We've loved each other so well.

And now it is time for me to drive to be by her side, to properly sit shiva with her family. I will offer them the cake, knowing the flavor doesn't matter. But I'm here.

And she is not alone. And we will get through this grief, together.

Violet's Apple Cake

My mom used to make this apple cake for all sorts of occasions. She'd double the recipe when company was coming over and serve it for dessert. The next day, we'd have it at breakfast. Later on, it's a wonderful companion to an afternoon cup of coffee. She'd take it to church potlucks and make it for new moms. It's the perfect "from scratch" recipe: easy, versatile, and delicious.

SERVES 8 TO 10

For the topping

1 tablespoon melted butter
1/2 cup firmly packed brown sugar
1/2 cup walnuts, chopped (still a bit chunky, not too fine)
1 teaspoon ground cinnamon
2 teaspoons all-purpose flour

For the cake batter

1 cup granulated sugar
1/4 teaspoon salt
1 teaspoon baking soda
1 1/2 cups all-purpose flour
1/4 teaspoon baking powder
1/2 cup vegetable oil
1/2 cup milk
2 eggs
1 teaspoon vanilla extract
2 cups Granny Smith apples, peeled and sliced, cut into 1-inch wedges

For the topping

1. In a small bowl, add the butter, brown sugar, walnuts, cinnamon, and flour. Mix together until the topping resembles coarse crumbs, and set aside.

For the cake batter

1. Preheat the oven to 350 degrees. Grease a 9 x 13-inch pan, and set aside.
2. In a large mixing bowl, add the sugar, salt, baking soda, flour, and baking powder. Mix with a fork to combine.
3. To the dry mixture, add the oil, milk, eggs, and vanilla extract. Beat on low speed until the mixture is smooth.
4. Add the apples to the mixture. Use a spatula to gently mix them into batter.

5. Pour the batter into the cake pan, spreading the apples evenly. Sprinkle the topping over the batter.
6. Bake at 350 degrees for 45 minutes. The cake is done when an inserted toothpick comes out clean.

23

We'll Be Your Family on Christmas Eve

MELANIE DALE

I am an initiator. As a lifetime member of the Put-Yourself-Out-There Club, which I'm sure a fellow initiator started, I've found myself in countless moments staring at a clock, or a door, or a chair across a table, desperately hoping people would show up to whatever thing I'd planned.

From before I heard Hayley Mills sing "Let's Get Together," I've dreamed of the fun I could share with others. My extroverted self loves a roomful of people I know who are meeting each other, enjoying themselves, and/or making a difference in the world. This has led to grand plans such as Karts for Kids, a shorter-than-I-hoped golf cart parade to raise money for orphaned and vulnerable children; Halloween Glow & Flow, a yoga class with glow sticks and more posable skeletons than yogis; and both my husband, Alex's, and my thirtieth birthday parties, when my desire to have big bashes for our births butted up against our dearth in friends.

Why am I like this? Because I am an initiator. Can't stop, won't stop. Seriously, I can't, even if I really, really want a break from the planxiety.

One year, as I got to know the neighbors and realized that a lot of people celebrated the holidays far from home, I decided to invite them all to our house for Christmas Eve. Christmas is a time for family, but not everybody lives near family. We live in a neighborhood with people from all over the world. We have Midwesterners and Middle Easterners. We have neighbors from India, Indiana, and beyond. Most people in our neighborhood are far from family.

You don't have family nearby? We'll be your family on Christmas Eve.

At least, that was my heart behind inviting tons of people over the night before a major holiday. Then the doubts began to creep into my brain. *Are people busy with their own traditions? Do they all go out of town for Christmas? Would guests want to stay in their jammies? What if everybody's at church instead? What about the people who don't celebrate Christmas? Did I just offend people with a party for Jesus?*

You don't get to choose your family, but you do get to choose your friends, so no one was obligated to come to my house on Christmas Eve, whether by DNA or a judge's signature. I wondered if anyone would show up.

I borrowed extra Crock-Pots and quadrupled my chili recipe, browning meat, opening cans, dumping ingredients together, plugging in pots, and setting them to low heat, then ran upstairs to get ready. On the way out the door for church, I looked around the kitchen, checking the Crock-Pots one last time, then climbed into the car.

We headed to Christmas Eve service and after, oh, I don't remember, "Mary Did You Know?" or some funky version of "The Little Drummer Boy"—*a-rum-pa-pum-pum rum-pa-pum-pum*—we drove home, and butterflies fluttered around my stomach.

We walked in and the smell of chili wafted to the door. My Crock-Pots had burbled like magic cauldrons while I sang carols and tried to keep my kids from dripping candle wax on the church carpet.

The clock hit six, and I flew around the kitchen, setting out ladles and bowls full of shredded cheddar and sour cream.

Alex looked around and said, "That's a lot of chili."

Yep. We'd be eating it for the next year if nobody showed up. I glanced at the clock.

The moment my dumb initiator heart keeps forcing me through had arrived. Like when you're on a roller coaster and you've climbed and climbed to the highest point, then start to crest the hill. You hang there for a moment before taking the plunge. Staring at the clock in an empty house is the roller-coaster hang.

Ding-dong!

Now, the plunge.

I made myself take a breath before rushing to the front door and flinging it open. "Merry Christmas!"

Neighbors crowded on the porch holding platters of food, and more walked up the driveway. People walked over from around the cul-de-sac and drove in golf carts from down the street. Our Christmas Eve family was here.

In the next few minutes our driveway and cul-de-sac filled with golf carts. In my neighborhood, you know it's a party when you see golf carts lined up along the street, families snuggled in blankets like a Georgia version of a sleigh ride.

Nearly everyone I invited showed up with food to share. I hadn't even told people to bring food. I wanted to feed people and spare them from cooking, but my neighbors are generous people and incredible cooks. Every surface in my kitchen was crowded with the most delicious fare. Ethiopian, Indian, gluten-free chocolate pretzels in the shape of reindeer, turkey pinwheels for the kids to grab, baked potatoes, cornbread, and of course, Christmas cookies. So many cookies. People brought whatever they had to share.

My house had never felt so full and warm. Our basement TV ran Christmas movies for the kids, and people spread out all over the house.

Every room filled with friends and neighbors catching up and eating chili out of paper bowls.

Oh my gosh, it *worked*. We've hosted the party ever since, a decade and change by now. Same neighbors (and some new ones) and same chili recipe (and some new ones).

Yes, we've added new chilis over the years, but the tried-and-true original still reigns supreme. When I was growing up, my aunt made it for us on Christmas Eves at my grandparents' house, and there's a secret ingredient that will either delight or frighten the weak, but there's no time to be overly precious when the world's best chili is at stake.

My chili doesn't begin like a scene from a Hallmark Christmas movie or a cooking show on Food Network. My chili fits better on SyFy or Shudder. Let me set the scene: The alien entrails dangle over the cavern below, clinging to the sides of the metal tube. One by one, the ropey guts lose their fight against gravity, until finally, with a loud *slurp*, the ball of viscera tumbles out.

Ker-plop!

And so begins my favorite family recipe, featuring a can of Campbell's spaghetti, formerly known as Franco-American Spaghetti before it was bought by Campbell's and rebranded a few years after I got married. Yes, a *can* of spaghetti. Saucy pasta suspended in a metal tube, shelf stable for longer than the preschool years, and that's saying something.

My chili is tasty, but what makes it truly special is the people eating it together at our annual Christmas Eve party.

We've hosted the party for so long that some of the kids who used to jump around in our basement are now college kids returning for the holidays. There are grown babies and new babies, and friends bringing their parents when they're in town. We combine families, our dads and moms sharing stories and everyone filled with Christmas cheer and chili beans. I love to see the conversations form, a group of high schoolers laughing in one room, and in another, some college kids reconnecting and sharing stories of dorm life and study abroad.

When Big Virus descended and we couldn't gather together indoors, I still made chili and texted a few of our Christmas Eve regulars. I loaded up the golf cart with individual containers of chili and toppings, and my whole family piled on—Alex and me in the front seat, and all three nearly grown kids squished into the back seat. We drove from house to house on the golf cart, delivering chili. At each house, friends took our chili and handed us other courses to share with everyone, so by the end of the golf cart ride, we'd distributed a full meal. We all ate separately, but we waved from porches and texted our Christmas cheer.

The following year, I started chemo days before Christmas Eve. Our neighbors didn't want us to cancel, so they carried the torch and hosted it in their driveway, chili al fresco. After a difficult day dealing with some of the worst chemo side effects, I wasn't sure I could make it. I knew everyone would understand if I stayed home, but I couldn't miss my favorite tradition.

I took a shower and slid on soft clothes. Hobbling across the cul-de-sac, down the golf cart path, and into our neighbors' driveway, I saw a long folding table covered in Crock-Pots. Beautiful. I made a beeline for a camp chair and sank into it with relief.

Heads turned and it was a record-scratch moment. I could tell my cancer just got real for my friends and their kids, who'd never seen me that sick.

Merry Christmas! We're mortal! My hair follicles are dying while I force down this chili!

In spite of my personal season, I relished sharing the Christmas season with the people I love, to see this tradition I'd started continue and thrive, without needing me to keep it going.

The next year, it was back at my house. But the party doesn't work because of where it is, what people bring, or what they wear. It works because it's simple. No more planxiety for this initiator, at least one day of the year.

I love it more than Christmas morning, which has always brought a level of expectation and performance with gift-giving. The Christmas Eve party is come-as-you-are. It's the annual check-in, when everyone is together, they can bring whoever and whatever to share, and the chili recipe is so easy that it practically makes itself. Over the years I've added a chicken enchilada chili recipe, and sometimes a gluten-free and vegan one. But my family's chili, the one I grew up with, is the one I return to, year after year. It's easy to remember, and you can double, triple, quadruple it without doing hard math.

You don't always know you're creating a tradition until you're in it. That first year, a house full of people, everyone's kids tangled up watching movies, eating cookies, people crammed around tables, and Crock-Pots galore, my neighbor turned to me and said, "Next year?"

> **You don't always know you're creating a tradition until you're in it.**

And we've never stopped. We'll host it for as long as neighbors keep coming and Campbell's keeps making spaghetti in a can.

"We'll Be Your Family" Chili

Some recipes are so simple and you make them for so long that they become part of you. The page in my family cookbook with this recipe is stained and written on, but I haven't needed it for years. When I head to the grocery store, I know which aisles to hit and what to grab to whip up a batch. This recipe is easy to double or triple. For my Christmas Eve party, I sextuple it and split it between two slow cookers, opening and pouring the cans like I'm a fancy bartender or barista. I like it with beef, but have made it plenty of times with ground turkey—tastes great either way.

MAKES 4 TO 6 SERVINGS

1 pound ground beef, browned and drained
1 can diced tomatoes
1 can chili beans
1 can Campbell's Spaghetti
Chili powder to taste
Cheddar cheese and sour cream for serving, optional

1. In a large Crock-Pot, add the cooked ground beef, diced tomatoes, chili beans, canned spaghetti, and chili powder, and stir together.
2. Turn the heat on low and cook for 3 or 4 hours.
3. Serve with cheddar cheese, sour cream, and any other toppings you'd like.

Note: Any chili beans work in this recipe. I prefer pinto beans in mild chili sauce, but this recipe can be made with kidney beans and at any heat level you like.

24

Perfect Strangers

MOLLY FLINKMAN

The story about how I ended up with nine strangers in my house for Thanksgiving starts a year and a half earlier—in a park on a warm June day.

I was eight months pregnant, pushing my two daughters on a tire swing, when I met a woman whose husband was a new medical resident in our city. My husband was also a new medical resident, so we chatted there for a while, connecting about all the things we had in common. The chance to talk to someone who spoke the same language as me felt like a life raft. She understood the particular loneliness that came from being on my side of unpredictable hospital schedules. She knew what it felt like to pack up and move across the country for a dream that belonged to someone else. The conversation buoyed me. It brought fresh air into my lungs.

Before I left, she introduced me to the other women she was with—a whole group of medical wives, gathered for a playdate. I went home and joined their Facebook group, hopeful I might see them again.

Six weeks later, our baby was born, and one of those wives reached out—she'd seen the announcement on Facebook—and told me their group wanted to bring me some meals.

Over the next week, five women walked hot meals across my front porch. I had met most of them that day at the park, but one woman introduced herself for the first time as she handed me a hot pan of fajitas. I was stunned by this kindness and moved by the group's willingness to help a family they didn't really know.

About a year later, our family drove west across Interstate 80, to spend a long weekend with my in-laws. My husband, Jake, was behind the wheel, and our kids—four years old, two years old, and ten months old—were spread throughout the back seats. We were making good time and set to arrive for dinner when we passed a family pulled over on the side of the road with a popped hood. Jake watched them as we drove by and paused in thought.

"I'm going to see if they need help," he told me.

Then he took the next available exit and began to circle back. Meanwhile, I silently assessed the inside-the-van situation. Our general rule for road trips was to *keep moving* because the kids usually noticed when we stopped. I cataloged every stall tactic available to me, but knew the movies and extra snacks were only as useful as our kids would allow them to be. When we pulled up behind the stalled sedan, I met Jake's eyes with my own, and he read my thoughts perfectly.

He looked at the kids in the back seats. "They'll be fine," he said. "I'll be right back."

Two hours later, he came back.

The car had blown its alternator, and Jake, a bit of a jack-of-all-trades, was able to help them replace the entire thing. The kids and I had been mostly fine for those two hours, thanks to all the extra snacks and a re-showing of *Frozen*, but I struggled to unfurrow my eyebrows when he returned to our van. I tried to have a good attitude—really, I did—but I was bored and uncomfortable and overstimulated by the constant back-seat demands.

Jake read my thoughts again. He told me how grateful the family had been for his help and thanked me for staying with the kids.

"I know it was inconvenient," he said. "But I want our kids to know that sometimes it's good to be inconvenienced for the sake of another person—even if you don't know who they are."

That brings us to the nine strangers who ended up in my home later that fall.

Jake was still in the thick of his medical residency. He had been scheduled to work a night shift on Thanksgiving, so I made plans to spend the holiday with a friend whose husband would also be at the hospital. One afternoon, while I consulted the internet about how exactly to roast a turkey—I'd never cooked a proper Thanksgiving meal on my own before—I saw a new comment in the Facebook group of medical wives.

The commenter had just moved to our city, and her husband was in his first year of medical school. He was planning to study for a test on Thanksgiving (a normal medical school thing), and because she was so far away from any family or friends, she bemoaned the fact that, for the first time in her life, she would have to spend the day alone with her two little boys.

I read her post and felt an immediate conviction to invite her to spend the day with us. This was quickly followed by some reasonable hesitations: I didn't know anything about her. I didn't know anything about her kids. I had three little kids, plus my friend's two little kids, which already felt like *so many little kids* for our small home to handle. Also (and maybe most importantly?) I didn't even know how to cook a turkey yet.

But then I remembered what it had felt like during Jake's first six months of residency, when I knew no one in our city. I remembered the way I used to stare at my phone and will it to ring or buzz with a text message. I remembered buckling our girls into their car seats and driving around town because I didn't know what else to do or where to go.

I remembered the way that simple conversation at the park had lifted me up. So I did what I would have wanted someone to do for me: I took a deep breath and told her she was welcome to spend Thanksgiving in our home.

"I'm going to roast my very first turkey like a real adult," I added.

She accepted—gratefully—and then told me she might try to trick her husband into coming over for dinner, too. A few days later, she asked if another medical couple she knew could come with their three kids. I did the math. Jake would join us for dinner in between waking up and leaving for his night shift, which meant we'd have seven adults and ten kids in a house without a dining room.

It'll be fine, I told myself. *It'll probably be fine.* And then I regretted my invitation every single day after I extended it.

I wished I could get back the cozy Thanksgiving with my friend and her kids. I worried the day would be too loud and chaotic. I wondered why I had invited this woman to spend the entire day with us. I secretly hoped one of my kids might get sick so I could call the whole thing off.

Still, the day approached, so I made the best plans I could. I assembled every extra chair I could find and made a plan for a second table in the basement. I wrote out a menu, bought a roasting pan, and hoped Martha Stewart knew what she was talking about when it came to cheesecloth and turkey. And all the while I tried to view the whole ordeal as an opportunity to practice the kind of hospitality our family valued.

I managed to get the turkey in the oven on Thanksgiving, but when my new internet friend walked into my house, the cheesecloth was burning and our smoke detectors chirped intermittently. We greeted one another, and as it turned out, she was a bit of a turkey expert. She took it upon herself to take over the roasting, and I did not stand in her way. Once the food was under control, we settled the kids into the basement playroom and tried to find things to talk about. The conversation was stilted and full of silent pauses. She was really lovely—delightful to be around—and also, it turned out, we just weren't destined to be fast friends.

The day passed slowly. Her friends showed up just before dinner, and her husband managed to pop over around the same time. Once all ten kids were present, the volume level of the house increased substantially, so Jake woke up looking especially tired. We made plates and ate turkey I could take almost no credit for. At some point before dessert, I found a boy drawing on my living room wall with crayons. They left about an hour after all my energy was gone.

I ended the day alone on my couch with a piece of pumpkin pie. I hadn't eaten any earlier because I knew I wanted to savor my slice in the quiet of the basement—a moment I planned before the turkey was even carved. I spread the whipped cream with my fork and then ate it slowly. At some point while I sat there in complete silence, my phone pinged with a Facebook message: *Thanks so much for having us! Hopefully it wasn't too crazy for you!*

And that was that. She didn't say much more, and I never saw her or any of them ever again. If I didn't have a picture to prove it all happened, I might think the whole thing was some kind of late-fall fever dream.

> **The grace of hospitality is no small thing, and those memories are enough to spur me on in this way of living.**

I don't know the true impact of that day—what exactly sharing the holiday meant to these families or how they carried the experience forward. I don't know how that Thanksgiving lives in their memories, but I do know how that day in the park lives in mine. I know how it feels to be on the outside of belonging and also what it means when a hand reaches in. The grace of hospitality is no small thing, and those memories are enough to spur me on in this way of living.

I'll never do it perfectly—goodness knows there are countless invitations or simple conversations I've talked myself out of entirely—but I will keep trying. I'll continue to give my phone number to moms I meet in lobbies or school hallways, and I'll invite people into our home whether or not I know them well. I will pray for eyes that see, and I'll scan sidelines, grocery store aisles, and, yes, even comment sections for the needs of those around me. I'll slow down. I'll turn around if necessary. I'll do my best to lean in even if it costs me something—even if the walls get drawn on with crayons.

How will you spend your life? I'll continue to ask myself. *What kind of stranger will you be?*

Easy, Breezy Greek Chicken Bowls

*It is my belief that everyone should have a couple of go-to meals when it comes to bringing food to new moms, and this is one of mine. It's fresh, full of delicious flavors, and—best of all—*requires no cooking. *You just need a grocery list and twenty minutes to shred chicken and chop some vegetables.*

MAKES 1 MEAL TO DELIVER TO A GRATEFUL FAMILY

1 or 2 store-bought, rotisserie chickens, (depending on how many people you're feeding)
2 cucumbers, chopped
2 (10-ounce) containers cherry tomatoes, sliced in half
Juice of 2 lemons
Salt and pepper to taste
1 container hummus
1 container tzatziki
1 container feta cheese
1 small jar kalamata olives
Pita bread
2 to 4 bags microwaveable rice or quinoa
2 plastic containers

1. Shred the chicken and place it in a plastic container.
2. In the second plastic container, combine the cucumbers, cherry tomatoes, lemon juice, and salt and pepper.
3. Deliver the chicken, seasoned vegetable mixture, hummus, tzatziki, feta cheese, kalamata olives, microwavable rice, and pita bread.
4. Tell the family to assemble their own individual chicken bowls however they want and make sure they keep the containers. (Because new moms don't need to keep track of where all that plasticware needs to be returned!)

Benediction

KIMBERLY KNOWLE-ZELLER

May our lives be one of
good company,
after we've been fed,
and we've shared stories,
and we've listened and been
listened to.

We've bared our souls
and heard the refrain—
Me too,
You're not alone,
We'll get through this,
I see you.

There's been hearty laughter
and maybe some tears,
connection on the couch,
blankets on our laps,
hot coffee steaming,
the gift of looking friends in
the eye,
and reaching out a hand to hold.

In the passing of sourdough
loaves,
chips and guacamole,
wine or water,
we've feasted and forgotten
about time,
been present with each other,
with phones out of sight,
for we know that these
gatherings,
these moments of friendship,
these meals and sharing,
are indeed holy ground.

We've traded recipes and book
recommendations,
our favorite tips to keep the
germs away,
that mascara and lip liner that
everyone compliments,
the links to wooden blocks
and Magna-Tiles

that keep the kids occupied for
hours.

Now take it all in—
the stories, connection, laughter,
and joy,
and keep opening doors
and hearts
set the extra places at the table,
make the phone call,
write that letter,
tell the neighbors: *you're
welcome here*
so that our lives will be one
of good company.

May your life be filled with
friends who laugh
and hold your hand when
doubt creeps in,
where homes are not places of
competition but comfort
and care,
where couches and front
porches become beacons
of hope,
where piles of laundry and
crumb-filled tables are
blessed signs of love.

May your life be one of good
company,
where doubts and struggles
are held,
where there is always room
to share
and enough to go around.

May your life be one of good
company,
where you are safe, known,
encouraged, and loved.

Acknowledgments

Annie Dillard once wrote, "Why are we reading, if not in hope of beauty laid bare, life heightened and its deepest mystery probed?"[1]

We are forever grateful—brought to tears even—to have been given the opportunity to share our stories with the world, to lay so much ordinary beauty bare, and to probe our deepest mysteries with the kindest readers on the planet. A gigantic, unyielding, heartfelt thank-you to everyone who has read our essays, bought our books, and otherwise supported our creative work throughout the years.

We are still writing because of you.

Notes

Chapter 1: A Few Simple Ingredients

1. Ann Hood, *Kitchen Yarns: Notes on Life, Love, and Food* (W. W. Norton, 2019), 81.

Chapter 3: Once Upon a Time

1. Janet Barton, "No-knead Crusty Bread," *Simply So Good,* September 19, 2018, updated June 16, 2020, https://www.simplysogood.com/crusty-bread/.

Chapter 6: Good Mothers Bake from Scratch and Other Lies I've Been Told

1. Laura Shapiro, *Something from the Oven: Reinventing Dinner in 1950s America* (Penguin Publishing Group, 2004), 73.
2. Spherical Insights LLP, "Global Cake Mixes Market Size to Exceed USD 2.19 Billion By 2033, news release, accessed March 28, 2024, https://www.globenewswire.com/news-release/2024/03/28/2853806/0/en/Global-Cake-Mixes-Market-Size-To-Exceed-USD-2-19-Billion-By-2033-CAGR-Of-3-5.html.
3. Shapiro, *Something from the Oven*, 79.

Chapter 7: The Best of Both Worlds

1. Justin Whitmel Earley, *Habits of the Household: Practicing the Story of God in Everyday Family Rhythms* (Zondervan, 2021), 53–54.
2. Heather Turner, "Chicken Tikka Masala," *Gourmet DIY Shanghai*, January 7, 2013, https://gourmetdiyshanghai.blogspot.com/2013/01/chicken-tikka-masala.html.

Chapter 14: Some Things Can't Be Rushed

1. *Complete Charcuterie: Over 200 Contemporary Spreads for Easy Entertaining* (Cider Mill Press, 2022), 131.

Chapter 15: The Proof Is in the Show Notes

1. Daniel Asa Rose, "Radical Hope and Laughter: An Interview with Anne Lamott," *Lit Hub*, November 9, 2018, https://lithub.com/radical-hope-and-laughter-an-interview-with-anne-lamott/.

Chapter 17: Collateral Damage

1. J. R. R. Tolkien, *The Hobbit*, revised edition (Ballantine Books, 1966), 11.
2. Tim Chester, *A Meal with Jesus: Discovering Grace, Community, & Mission Around the Table* (Crossway, 2011), 49.

Chapter 19: Cocoon

1. Danielle Walker, *Against All Grain: Delectable Paleo Recipes to Eat Well and Feel Great* (Victory Belt Publishing, 2013), 130.

Chapter 21: Same Script, Different Cast

1. "Curry-Scented Butternut Squash Soup," *The Pampered Chef*, accessed May 7, 2025, https://www.pamperedchef.com/recipe/Main+Dishes/Curry-Scented+Butternut+Squash+Soup/15659.

Acknowledgments

1. Annie Dillard, *The Writing Life* (Harper & Row, 1989), 72.

About Coffee + Crumbs

People offer mothers a lot of advice. We offer stories instead.

Coffee + Crumbs is a beautiful online journal filled with hundreds of stories about motherhood. At the core of our space, we want mothers to feel safe, known, encouraged, and loved.

Visit www.coffeeandcrumbs.net to learn more.

Contributors

Adrienne Garrison
Ashlee Gadd
Becky Morquecho
Callie Feyen
Cara Stolen
Katie Blackburn
Kimberly Knowle-Zeller
Melanie Dale
Molly Flinkman
Neidy Hess
Ruth Gyllenhammer
Sarah J. Hauser
Sonya Spillmann

Photography by Jennifer Floyd